THE COWSLIP YEARS

By the same author:

GRAIN AND CHAFF

The Cowslip Years

A country boyhood remembered
by
W.E. DRAYCOTT M.B.E.

* * *

Sketches by Karin Sharp

First published in 1989
by Ouse Publications

Typeset in 11/12 pt Times Roman by
The Castlefield Press Ltd.,
Wellingborough, Northants

Printed and bound by
Woulnough Bookbinding Ltd.,
Irthlingborough, Northants

Ouse Publications,
6 High Street,
Bozeat, Northants

ISBN 0 9510725 1 X

To
The Teversal Girls

CONTENTS

1

SETTING THE SCENE

I wonder do the mice still play football above the ceiling of my old bedroom on winter nights, dribbling their hazel-nuts around the roof space? Perhaps the moon peeps through some cobwebbed attic window to find a brittle, yellowed copy of the *Magnet*, with tales of the Greyfriars boys and their jolly japes. They say the old mill is gone, but is the cherry tree still there by the stream, offering its summer clusters of sweet, red fruit? At least the cowslips must return each spring, to delight the eye and provide early nectar for the bees.

The venue for these musings lies where the busy motorway threads its way northwards between Chesterfield and Mansfield, for immediately to the east nestles a peaceful oasis of countryside virtually unaffected by the mining area which surrounds it. There, folded within an elbow of the lane leading from Teversal to Pleasley stands Newbound Mill, a centuries-old farmstead with its pleasant views of orchard, stream and ancient bridge – the place where I enjoyed my boyhood years from seven till nearly twelve years of age.

My country idyll – for idyll it seems as viewed from sixty years and more on – is set in the 1920s, a time of national depression yet one in which, I believe, the general quality of life was more rewarding than disappointing. Ordinary folk worked so hard for their basic needs that such time and money as was left for leisure seemed to be better appreciated than by our selfish and greed-dominated society of today. I am well aware of the hardships suffered at that time, as over half of my school companions were the children of coal miners, and tenant farming on a shoestring was itself a tiring, far from lucrative and often heartbreaking way of making a living.

Of those who shared my home life at Newbound Mill Farm, originally we were five in family – father, mother, a teenaged sister, elder brother and myself, with a baby sister arriving later. Additionally there was the live-in farm-hand who was virtually also one of the family, as were the dogs and cats. I cannot exclude the farm animals and poultry either, as the relative isolation of the farm meant that I would often turn to them for companionship.

Having outlined the countryside, my home and my family, I must mention also Teversal village, for there I wrestled both with the Three Rs and the Devil, as I attended the school and church there. This involved a near-two-mile walk each way down a narrow, winding lane through truly English countryside. The village was (and still is) small and sleepy, the church picturesquely medieval and the church school typically Victorian, of a size barely sufficient for its forty or so pupils. Those children were rather a hotchpotch lot, drawn from the village itself, the nearby mining community and a few outlying farms and cottages.

So that sets the scene for my early boyhood days –

countryside, farmstead home, family and village school, plus of course the animals. It is the atmosphere of those times and surroundings that I hope to evoke for you, though I cannot promise to be over-fastidious at times in my choice of subject matter, for the truth must out!

2

FAMILY PEN-PORTRAITS

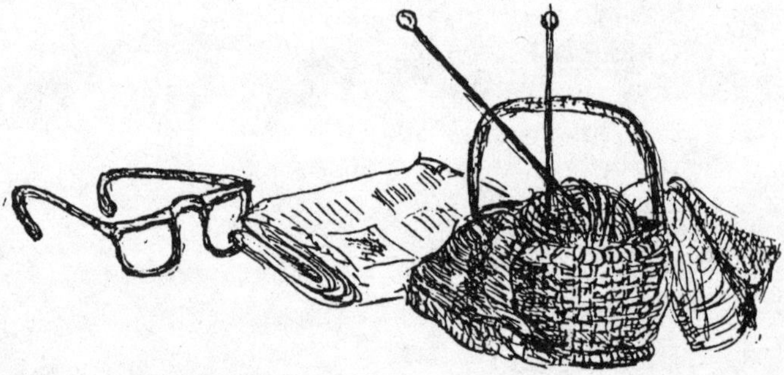

Enjoyable as Newbound Mill Farm was, I now realise that much of its engaging character sprang from the dilapidated quaintness of the place. Its run-down land, broken-down farm machinery, non-pedigree livestock and old fashioned methods all militated against achieving anything more than scratching a bare living from the soil. This all sprang from the character of my father Joseph Draycott, as likeable as the old place itself but whose over-trusting ways resulted in us being at Newbound instead of some more profitable farm. Personally I don't regret a thing, but for Father's sake I wish it had been otherwise.

He was short and lean, very active, painstaking and determined. His whereabouts around the farmstead were seldom in doubt for long, as his progress around barn, stable, cowshed and yard was marked by the bustling rattle of milk bucket, shouted instructions to Frank the farm-hand, or clatter of hobnailed boots on cobblestones. Work around the yard always seemed to involve buckets, and generally Father would be carrying one or often two, filled with water, milk, pig swill, bran mash, cow cake and the like, or even his jacket. Stop him to ask a question, and down would go the bucket while his cap would be pushed back for a contemplative scratch of the head. Giving thought to some questions required leaning with one hand against the nearest wall and chewing on some seed or stalk of hay, while the weatherbeaten, moustached face stared intently at the ground. Sometimes a stub of pencil and grubby scrap of envelope was fished from his breeches pocket for some rough-and-ready reckoning – not always easy, as his education had stopped before the age of twelve. This is no slur on my father, but evidences the fact that his lack of book-learning coupled with an easy going nature made him a prime target for any con-man.

Father had spent some years working in Canada and returned home in 1910 to marry and start on his own as a tenant farmer. Sure enough, after a few years that con-man turned up in the form of a relative by marriage, borrowed Father's hard-earned capital and soon spent it all on the fast life of a self-styled gentleman farmer. Hence our family move from a reasonably prosperous farm to dear old down-at-heel Newbound Mill.

However, there was still satisfaction to be had in the battle of experience against wind, weather, and the other factors more under human control. Father would walk the fields to check the soil with kicks of heel or toe, pluck an ear of wheat to sample for ripeness, or glance around to assess the weather. Decisions would follow, implemented by calls for plough, roller, wagon etc. as required.

In the evenings he would often fall asleep in his high-backed armchair, with off-the-peg spectacles askew and a copy of the *Farmer & Stockbreeder* lying part-scanned on floor or lap. Perhaps he was back in Canada, enjoying maple syrup pancakes in some prairie farm kitchen down Manitoba

way.

He seldom lost his temper or strong sense of humour, and such physical punishment as my brother and I received at his hands was often at Mother's instigation. Clear in my mind is the fact that so many people have used the same word in their assessment of him – they called him a gentleman.

A portrait of my mother, as Sarah Ann Elliott, before her marriage, shows an attractive young Edwardian lady. She differed from Father in several respects, being of a somewhat less liberal and rather sterner nature, though as decent, honest and hardworking as he was. Above average height and of ample though not stout build, she aimed to have her own way, quietly if possible but more forcibly if necessary. Nevertheless she had her warmer side, enjoying all aspects of her social life and often taking a leading and vigorous part in various functions.

I believe her character derived largely from my grandmother, who I remember as a rather stern person. The old lady had kept a village shop when younger, while grandfather had owned one of the last wind-driven corn mills, but he died too early for me to have any recollection of him.

There are two or three pictures of Mother that come most readily to mind: I see her plump backside protruding as she bent before an open oven door, her face flushed from the searing gusts of heat; then I see the wiping of hands on apron, accompanied by a quick sniff as she turned a disapproving back on some situation or remark; and I recall her healthy laughter when something amused her, for in spite of everything she had a good sense of humour when she chose to let it off the lead.

I suppose the key to Mother lay in her strict upbringing, when Victorian virtues were paramount; this was reflected in a large picture hanging prominently on the wall, showing several biblical scenes including *The Prodigal Son, The*

Widow's Mite, The Wise and the Foolish Virgins, etc.

Her industry was nothing short of amazing, for in addition to running the family home of three adults and (latterly) four children, with all that entails in the way of cooking, cleaning, washing and ironing, mending, bed-making etc., she would regularly help out with the lighter farm work and carry baskets of eggs and butter for sale around the area. On top of all this she was a very active member of the local chapel and Womens Institute, made social calls on various neighbours, and undertook tiresome bus journies to visit the several relatives spread around Nottinghamshire, Leicestershire and Lincolnshire. When preparing to set out on her travels she exhibited a rather strange physical squeamishness, for while inserting the hatpin through hat and hair she would wince and hiss with a sharp intake of breath, steeling herself for the grazed scalp which probably never came.

In spite of her daunting programme of domestic and social activities, she scarcely ever seemed to tire, sometimes even stepping in to bolster Father's confidence when fatigue made him despondent. Her stern shrewdness also came in useful from time to time, steering him clear of the pitfalls into which his good nature would otherwise have led him. She was a loyal wife, a caring mother and the dominant force in the family.

Big sister Hilda's five-year start on me, coupled with her sex, rather reduced any overlapping of our respective orbits. However, when these did cross there were more gentle bumps than spark-emitting clashes, for she had inherited more of the Draycott warmth than the Elliott dominance. As the teenager that she then was, she was darkly attractive with a fresh complexion and the cuddly lingerings of puppy fat.

Hilda left school shortly after we moved to Newbound, and then helped Mother with the housework, though one

would not think so from the verbal discord which often echoed around the house. Surprisingly Mother did not get things all her own way, as teenage rebellion was setting in and even the Draycott tolerance can only stand so much. The only time I remember Mother being driven to tears was when an acrid smell from the oven signalled Hilda's alleged negligence in letting the milk pudding burn, with nothing left but a dish of carbonised rice and lactose.

Fortunately Hilda found an outlet in the local Girls' Friendly Society and the name 'G.F.S.' still rolls easily from even my own tongue, as I heard her use it so often and affectionately. There she found someone who proved to be a lifelong friend and confidante – the attractive and personable Lily. One of my memories is of Hilda and Lily seated together in the spacious window of my bedroom, high up in the old house. As they sewed and indulged in eager girl-talk chat, they would glance down and across the orchard to the wide bridge where youths from Pleasley would sometimes congregate. On that particular occasion they titillated their fantasies by asking me searching questions on my own youthful romances, giggling loudly at the coyness of my replies.

Much of Hilda's spare time when at home was taken up by such things as reading the *Girls' Own Paper*, a little non-virtuoso piano-playing, evenings devoted to dressmaking, and no doubt looking ahead to when she might get married.

Undoubtedly my elder brother Philip was the blue-eyed boy both physically and by parental preference. Luckily a scarcely concealed undercurrent of brotherly rivalry between us was offset by a good rapport, and throughout life we enjoyed other's company and respected one another's talents and achievements. That sibling jealousy must have been aroused in Philip quite early on, for I was only two when he pushed one of my fingers between the rollers of a wooden clothes mangle while he turned; my finger was indeed mangled, for the scar both shows and makes itself felt to this day.

Philip was tallish, reasonably well built, good looking and endowed with a fair amount of charm. He was inclined to avoid physical confrontation by the use of diplomacy, having learned the ease with which most people can be manipulated by such means. Whereas Hilda was a Draycott with a little Elliott stiffening, Philip was basically an Elliott modified by Draycott characteristics. (Much later evidence of Phil's rather covert character came one day during the war, when I was a lunchtime guest at his Royal Navy establishment. His beetle-browed naval captain C.O. suddenly launched a verbal torpedo across the table at me with the question "Now, Mr Draycott, tell me what your brother is really like!").

My brother was regarded as more level-headed than myself, and proved more amenable to helping with odd jobs on the farm. In actual fact he disliked these chores just as much as I did, but had the sense to knuckle under and bide his time till ready to declare his hand. Like Hilda he took piano lessons, but with more polished results, and indeed music in general with the organ and piano in particular turned out to be his great love.

As to myself, it now falls on me to write my own character assessment, as I cannot readily think of anyone more suitable! Physically, I also was on the tall side, but of slight build though wiry. As to the ratio of genes received from my respective parents, here I will try and exercise a little diplomacy rather late in life by saying that I am probably a fifty-fifty mixture of Draycott and Elliott. (All in favour? Carried!). I was in fact christened Walter Elliott Draycott, born at Long Bennington in Lincolnshire during a zeppelin raid, though I could not truthfully claim that to be one of my recollections.

I am told that I wore extraordinarily large boots, but as I

am still tall but only take a size seven shoe, I can only assume that those seven-league boots were either an insurance against equally extraordinary rapid growth, or that they were brother Phil's cast-offs. Certainly I wore short corduroy trousers, as Mother considered they were hard-wearing, so they must have been.

I was very active, inventive, imaginative, impulsive and maverick. Predictably I developed a degree of resentment after several incidents when I took the blame for Philip's misdemeanours, and on one occasion decided to take prompt action. In spite of insisting that Phil was the guilty party, I was punished and immediately ran out into the dusk for some distance. Climbing a tree I settled down into a fork in the trunk to brood on yet one more injustice, determined to sit it out and shame those concerned into some form of apology. After possibly two hours of listening to my name being called by the worried search party, I let them off the hook by returning indoors. It transpired that Phil had finally admitted his guilt, so for a short while I received a kind of inverted Prodigal Son reception, though falling short of the complete fatted calf treatment. In retrospect I suppose it was a Pyrrhic victory for me, as it put the others in a humiliating position.

While not short of friends during school hours, at home I often had to rely on my own company or that of the pets and other animals, and was inclined to make my own amusement in a variety of ways. I was reasonably content to do this.

There was also that honorary member of the family, Frank the farm-hand. He was in his twenties, stocky, strong, loyal and cheerful. His family lived in my mother's native village and had been known to both my parents for many years. Frank was permanently and very markedly wry-necked, a condition said to be due to repeated neglect by his grandmother when laying him in his cot – a story readily believed at the time but which would now seem a little far fetched. He and I became good friends, and I would join him at work in the fields or farmyard whenever possible.

Finally there were the pets, who I suppose were as lucky as we were ourselves, living in the countryside with plenty of freedom and companionship, and not having to worry where their next meal would come from. To stick to protocol and present them in order of seniority, first came the ageing tortoiseshell cat Tittums, her ridiculous-sounding name being of dubious origin. I can never visualise her as being anything other than old, and seldom far from the hearth. Next came our jet black mongrel Jack, whose chief duty was that of guarding the home. He was a typical security man – identify yourself or else! The marmalade coloured collie bitch Gyp had other work to do, being an excellent sheep dog but who I considered to be a little too obsequious. Junior in age but quite aware of her chocolate-box beauty was the black persian cat Fluff, with her well-laundered white bib. I would call her a gold digger.

With that introduction to stage and cast, I can start my fairly random recollections of those never-to-return scenes of the 1920s.

3

THE DAILY ROUND

At Newbound Mill Farm, getting up at cock-crow literally meant just that; a half-dozen or so of those gaudy, arrogant birds would generally be cock-a-doodling one another around the area as the men bestirred themselves with milking-stool and bucket. A while before that, Father would have silenced the dented alarm clock, slipped in his false teeth and climbed up the back stairs to make sure that Frank was awake. Mother would follow downstairs to prepare breakfast in time for the men coming in when milking was over.

The subdued background noises of farmyard and house coming to life would gradually awaken Philip and myself, each sound identified as we drowsed on for a while: double click of barn door latch, muffled stamp of Gilbert the horse, Frank's "Move over!" to a cow, the rattle of poker in fire-grate – hundreds of clues as to the progress outside and below.

With all signs pointing to the right moment, we would leave our warm bed for a cat-lick wash, looking like a pair of Wee Willie Winkies in our long nightshirts. Cold water would be poured from the chipped, blue-and-white ewer into the (matching!) basin on the wash-stand. The face flannel might even be threatened with soap, and in winter there was the luxury of hot water brought up by Mother. A quick pulling-on of clothes, and we would clatter down the two flights of stairs which were carpetless until the landing below was reached and had a threadbare look even after that.

Breakfast was on everyone's mind, from the cat brushing its persuasive tail around Mother's ankles to the men arriving hungry after an hour's milking. Oatmeal porridge would have been prepared the night before and served up simmering hot from a glazed, brown stewpot, with milk fresh from the cows and sprinkled with brown sugar. As often as not there would be thick slices of cold, fat bacon to follow, cut from a flitch hanging from one of the hooks in the beamed ceiling. The family took their breakfast in the spacious living room, while through an open door Frank would be seated alone at the big kitchen table, chunks of greasy bacon apparently slipping down his gullet without the benefit of chewing. The cats Fluff and Tittums would share a saucer of milk on the kitchen hearth, while outside by his kennel, the black mongrel Jack would be wolfing-down his own breakfast of watered-down warm milk and stale bread.

Sometimes that cosy scene would be marred by apprehension, for it was not unknown to have gone to bed the previous night under the threat of "Just you wait until your Dad finds out in the morning!" This cloud would hang in the morning air until Father had arrived for breakfast and passed judgement on the alleged offence, when hopefully I would either be let off with a warning, or sentence would be deferred until the evening. With any luck he would then have had a good day or the matter would have been forgotten, submerged under more important preoccupations such as ploughing, sheep-shearing or the price of corn.

With breakfast over it was time for everyone to go their respective ways, the men to yard or field and we children to school, each with his packet of food and bottle or enamelled can of drink. Before Mother turned to her housework she might catch one of us as we left, in order to open the cumbersome wooden shutters which covered the windows. This was because she was very frightened of the bats which were in the habit of roosting behind the shutters, her fear stemming from the belief that their main ambition was to entangle themselves in women's hair.

I omitted to mention lighting of the fire before breakfast, as often it was damped down and left in overnight; however I can now back-track an hour and describe that operation, a thankless task overall though sometimes rewarded by a glow of self-satisfaction at a job well done. It was at Newbound Mill that I passed my firelighter's test and henceforward acted as second reserve in that respect. The process really started the night before, when kindling sticks would be left to dry in the oven, leaving the door ajar in case overheating resulted in the wood smouldering or even taking fire.

The downstairs morning light would show a cheerless situation, with cold grey ash piled to overflowing in the ashpan and spilling onto the hearth, while the grate above contained a mixture of ash and cinders. No amount of care in tipping the ash into a bucket could prevent an atomic cloud of the stuff ascending into the room's troposphere, revealing hitherto unseen shafts of light. This job done, and with the cinders separated for re-use, it was time to lay the fire. First came a sheet of the *Mansfield Reporter,* scanned quickly for any item of interest then loosely bunched as a base on which to build. Layers of the dried kindling came next, surmounted by smallish lumps of coal, every item selected and arranged according to past experience.

Time now to put things to the test, and with match applied to paper the five would soon reveal its intentions – to catch or not to catch, co-operation or stubborn refusal. Noise was a reliable clue, for a bright and lively crackling and spurting generally heralded success, whereas a quiet, sullen smouldering surely spelt failure and the need to go through the whole wretched business again. On the other hand, winning the battle brought an immediate uplift of spirits, and tidying up could proceed with a whistle and a kindly word for the cat.

Mention of the cat reminds me of a time when it was nearly brought to a painful and untimely end by the foregoing routine. One morning after breakfast, as Mother opened the oven door a furry black rocket shot past her and bolted shrieking out of the room. It transpired that the cat Fluff must have crept into the oven during the night, sleeping warm and snug beside the kindling. Fate decreed that whoever lit the fire in the morning removed the kindling and closed the oven door without noticing the snoozing cat, so Puss was left to sweat it out until delivered by chance. She was not seen for days, and there is no further recollection of her using the oven as one of the first centrally-heated bedrooms.

Mother's post-breakfast routine of housework generally seemed to begin with making the beds, and on non-school or non-Hilda days I might be called on to help. This was hard work, as the feather mattresses had to be pummelled, punched and thrown around to restore some degree of shape, like blowsy matrons at a turkish bath. Split seams were not infrequent, releasing flurries of minute feathers which appeared to be lighter than air, hanging around to exasperate the perspiring bedmaker by sticking to the face or lodging in ear and nose. Flock mattresses did not respond well to this roughing-up treatment, but Philip and I got to

know the relief-map features of our own few square feet of bed, avoiding its knobbly Peak Districts in favour of the more comfortable table-lands.

There were six bedrooms plus an apple loft, though only four were in use and furnished with the brass and iron bedsteads commonly used in those days. The railed bed-ends were surmounted with hollow brass knobs which could be unscrewed and used to imitate train noises by blowing across the top, or for hiding small items. This reminds me that as Mother moved around during bedmaking in our room, she would be unaware that she was brushing against my personal wall safe, for by an ingenious use of the wallpaper pattern I disguised the flap to a small cavity which I had scooped in the plaster. Inside were 'jewels' or coded messages, and I would lie in bed thrilled by the knowledge that I alone knew of this secret cache. On the subject of deception, those bedrooms provided an ideal ground for playing hide-and-seek, as they lay on two floors and could be reached from either end of the house, by the front or back stairs.

At Newbound Mill, Mother must have been sorely tempted to ignore the Victorian maxim that cleanliness is next to godliness, for attempts to keep the place clean must have been heartbreaking, but she never gave in. As the 'back' door perversely lay at the front, any visitor's first impressions were gained from the kitchen, hence its flagstoned floor, hearth, expanse of table-top and other salient features received priority at cleaning-up times. A temporary face-lift could be achieved by wet cloth, mop and duster, but if the day's schedule permitted, then the full treatment was given. After scrubbing the bare table, attention was transferred to the floor. Some forethought was needed here to avoid cutting oneself off, as tiptoeing back to dry land could spoil that lovely clean floor. The harsh rythm of brush and occasional rattle of bucket was sure to attract one of the cats, its tour of inspection making a trail of paw marks till sent scurrying off with the flick of a wet rag.

With hearth brushed free of cinders and steaming from a quick wipe over, the mantlepiece above could be dusted, lifting the box of 'England's Glory' matches and the 'Present from Skegness' ornament. At this stage, Mother would wipe her hands on her apron, cast an appreciative glance over her handiwork and then move on for a quick tidy-up of the other downstairs rooms.

Whatever other daily tasks might be put off, there was no escape from cooking, as men coming in hungry from barn or field did not like being fobbed off by cold fare. Unlike today, there was no take-away food shop round the corner and no wealth of convenience foods, so it was down to the basics of store room, cooking range and native culinary skills.

If the housewives of today receive compliments for tasty meals cooked with every modern aid, then surely those like my mother who coped with those old cooking ranges should get gold medals. The fire of our range heated a hot-water boiler on the left and an oven on the right, which sounds fairly elementary. However, together with its various bits, pieces and gadgets it had virtually the full capabilities of a modern electric oven. Properly used and humoured, this versatile bag of tricks could simmer, boil, grill, fry, bake, roast or toast, with a few extra acts thrown in, such as drying clothes, heating flat-irons and providing warmth and a low light for persons and pets alike.

To bring a shoulder of lamb, rabbit pie, egg custard or whatever to sizzling, mouth-watering perfection at the appointed hour, Mother had to function both as thermostat and timer. Like an organ player, by various push-pull manipulations and other tricks she produced Beethoven symphonies of roast beef and yorkshire pudding, Mozart minuets of apple tart, and Bach fugues of plum duff, from arrangements by Mrs Beeton.

A fixed time for the midday meal could not always be guaranteed, so arrangements would sometimes be made to inform the men in the fields via 'flags' hung from a bedroom window, like naval signals at Trafalgar. Thus a plain white towel might mean "Come and get it!", or a flapping pair of long-johns indicate "Unexpected delay. Watch this space."

If I was at home during cooking sessions, then occasionally these were little pleasures to be indulged in. Pastry making would mean left-over scraps of dough for moulding into shapes of pigs or men, with currants pressed in for eyes. The dough possessed the property of extracting hitherto unsuspected grime from my hands, so that swine and men went grey-faced and pudgy into the oven, though later emerging crisp and sun-tanned, ready to burn fingers and mouth by impatient sampling. At other times there would be tide-marks of congealed jam to be scraped off the inside of the heavy brass preserving pan, savouring every lick of the wooden spoon. Here there was a penalty awaiting, for tying-down of the jars involved holding my thumb on the knot, invariably with a painful trapping of flesh, though Mother seemed sadistically unmoved by my wincing.

The boiler which formed part of the range always had a ladle lying on top, wooden-handled to insulate the user. However, there was no protection for the unwary from scalding steam issuing from the boiler as the iron lid was hinged up. Water for topping-up the boiler came from a small hand-pump mounted over the stone sink in the kitchen, for there was no mains supply in this remote area. Hard frosts would penetrate the solid kitchen walls and freeze up this gallant little work-horse, calling for equally severe treatment with kettlefuls of boiling water and hot cloths. At such times the standby supply was a butt of rainwater outside the back door, though this first entailed cracking and lifting out a one-inch thick cartwheel of solid ice. That butt was also the source of water for swilling down the flagstoned area by the back door, when the splashing and brushing would force Jack the house dog to seek refuge in his kennel, with a rattle of chain against cast-iron water bowl.

Horses and cattle had a crystal-clear, depth-cool supply of spring water which flowed ceaselessly into a stone trough in the main farmyard, alongside the gates which opened onto the public road or lane. That spring water was famed throughout the neighbourhood, and miners from Pleasley would regularly help themselves to a drink from a chipped enamelled mug left there for that purpose, filling it from the snub-nosed lead spout which poked through the stone wall. A further supply of water for the animals came from the stream which flowed through the home fields and paddock.

The subject of water leads naturally on to sanitation – or should do, for as there was no piped water, so there was no mains sewage. Our little house at the bottom of the garden was known as 'the W', though water-closet it was not. At least it lent atmosphere to the place, and there was little need for visitors to ask where the loo was.

If the main punctuations of a normal day's routine were the full stops provided by meals, then one of the commas was the arrival of the postman. Very few homes had a telephone, and in any case no lofty brown poles carrying humming wires ran anywhere near Newbound Mill Farm, so it was a case of communicating by letter or not at all. Hence the postman's visit was almost a daily event, as there were not only the usual letters from friends and relatives to expect, but also exciting things like seed catalogues and livestock-medicine price lists. At least there was no junk mail, so the first sight of that uniformed figure approaching was welcomed, with the virtual certainty that he would bring something of interest.

Not only did that cheerful servant of the Crown deliver the mail in all weathers, he also formed a mobile clearing-house for local news and gossip, both gathering more and disseminating more as he made his rounds on foot. He also performed another useful function, for not until the year after we left the farm did we even own a wireless or crystal set, so he was often asked for the correct time, verified by reference to his chunky pocket watch.

There were times when the postman's call brought at least a temporary apprehension in the form of a telegram or black-edged envelope, as the former usually contained unwelcome news while the latter certainly spelt bereavement. But these occasions were the exceptions, for in general his visit was one of the most welcome highlights of the day.

As the daily routine progressed to lighting-up time, there was no flicking of switches, for electricity was still several light-years away from inclusion in the Draycott domestic scene, nor was gas available. Our forms of lighting in those days – oil lamps and candles – may not be efficient illuminators but they make up for that shortcoming by more lovable qualities. Their mellow glow softens harsh shadows, enhances pleasant features and flatters indifferent ones. Additionally, candles provide gentle diversions with their dancing shadow patterns, responding to the slightest change of air flow.

All this does not mean there was no dark side to those lights, for sometimes with a change of mood they could give faces an evil look, or the quick flit of shadow across a dark corner would suggest some unfriendly presence. Yet overall the dusk brought a homely, togetherness feeling as lamps were lit, shutters closed and curtains drawn, the precursors to a family evening together.

Some of the best times were winter nights, with roaring fires forcing us into a gradual widening of the fireside half-circle, edging-back chair, stool or cushion from the searing heat. Neither of the two cats would move until its fur began to scorch or a spark landed on it like a burning meteorite, sending it scampering under the table. The cosy feeling would be heightened by boisterous gusts of wind echoing in the chimney, or the lash of sleet like handfuls of gravel thrown against the shutters.

Each member of the family had his or her own way of passing the time, sometimes by choice but often of necessity. If Father did not fall asleep too early then he might occupy himself in a footwear-conditioning session, placing a saucer of mutton fat on the hearth to liquefy then rubbing it well into the leather and seams of his heavy farm boots, to both soften and waterproof them. That done, and if still sufficiently awake, a glance through the *Farmer & Stockbreeder* might follow, with its articles on new-fangled equipment he could never afford, or pictures of monstrous-sized bulls which made our own look like a ninety-seven-pound weakling from a chest-expander advert.

We others had our own reading material, Philip and I squabbling over whose turn it was for reading spiffing tales of eton-collared dudes in the *Magnet,* the consolation prize being a browse through the garish pages of *Tiger Tim's Weekly*, with its Noah's Ark gang of animals aping humans – parrots wearing spats and giraffes in knickerbockers etc. For sister Hilda it was the *Girl's Own Paper* where a jolly-hockey-sticks atmosphere prevailed, while the *Ladies Companion* favoured by Mother seemed to specialise in teacup-balancing curates being spurned by personable young schoolmistresses with other fish to fry. All good stuff!

In actual fact, Mother would more often be engaged in the constant battle of clothes repairs, ever button-sewing, patching and darning to keep the backlog within manageable proportions. More relaxed moments would find her knitting, the soothing click of needles and warmth of her lap hypnotizing the purring cat into a rythmic flexing of the paws; on one occasion a sudden eruption of that cosy scene sent cat, wool and knitting pattern flying as sharp claws hooked into Mother's thighs. She retreated to the privacy of the kitchen to apply Zambuk to the wound, while the skulking miscreant peeped from under the dresser, no doubt pondering on the strangeness of humans.

Mother would sometimes co-opt us into rug making, which entailed clipping discarded clothes into strips ready for threading through a backing made from sack-bag material. Thus suits, skirts and overcoats were preserved for posterity, their days of work or leisure, harvesting or weddings giving way to nights spent under shuffling feet or sleeping dogs.

In lighter mood Mother would suggest a game of cards, whist being her favourite. The astuter players were at a distinct advantage, as many of the dog-eared cards were as identifiable from the rear as from the front, while when pressed into service the joker's unworn smoothness made him stand out like a beacon. Ludo, Tiddly-winks and Snakes-and-ladders were also family favourites, though the last-named game both attracted yet repelled me by its brilliant vipers, pythons and anacondas, so that landing on one gave me the shudders.

Going to bed late was almost unheard of at Newbound Mill. The approach of bedtime was signalled by 'foddering up', when the men did their rounds of stable and cowsheds to see that the animals had enough food to chomp away at during the night. Basically this was to ensure stamina for the horses next morning and milk from the cows. That done, and with all the family indoors (cats and dogs excepted), bolts would be shot home and crudely-fashioned keys turned in old locks, as successive generations had done in that house since at least Elizabethan times, or even way before then.

We boys would be first upstairs, either singly or together depending on whether or not Philip had decided to scare me with ghost tricks on the way up. Such pranks were easy enough to pull off in the dark of those two flights of twisting stairs, with the eerie atmosphere of hooting owls and moaning wind. Equally scary was complete silence, not knowing from where he would leap out with a screech, or merely touch me from behind. This ordeal over, we would continue up to bed, where with any luck a stone hot-water bottle or heated brick in an old sock would have been slipped between the icy sheets.

Safely in bed and with the candle shedding tears of molten wax, a strong puff or two would bring sudden darkness, followed by a lingering smell of smouldering wick and candle grease. The day was over.

Before moving on to other things, a retrospective look over the household routine which I have just tried to describe prompts me to make the following observation. In the course of those daily rounds one would see and use a wide variety of furniture, goods and chattels, most of them cherished over the years yet few of them worth a second look should they have been laid out in a paddock for auction in those days. Times change, for put the clock on sixty years or so and offer those bits and pieces for sale today: Father would have had no problem in replacing his lost capital – with money to spare for modern substitute items.

4

SUNDRY OCCASIONS

The weekly round at Newbound Mill Farm started as at most other homely, god-fearing establishments – with Washday. To Mother it was written in stone that Monday was Washday (? from the Norse 'Woch', god of cleanliness!), so come rain or shine that meant an early start to get things under way.

By breakfast time the wash-house chimney would smoke-signal the fact that Washday had indeed started. Soon, the soiled linen earmarked for a carbolic gruelling was cast into the steaming, bubbling maelstrom of the hemispherical iron copper. Sheets were the most reluctant to stay submerged, surfacing like flatulent white whales until pushed under with the copper-stick, a bleached, truncheon-like device sometimes used for threatening myself or Philip.

A forceful to-and-fro swirling in the dolly-tub came next, whilst persistent offenders were given the rub-a-dub-dub treatment on a ridged wash-board. After rinsing free of grime, soap and scum, the washing was put through the wooden rollers of the mangle, the larger items ballooning like the throats of amorous bullfrogs.

Finally, cleansed of all sin the garments ascended as near to heaven as the prop could push up the clothes-line, shirts dancing merrily with chemises and long-johns flapping shyly alongside ladies' bloomers. Those last-named items had the voluminous appearance of a Grimaldi clown's pantaloons, and with the wisdom of a lifetime I now see them as designed specifically to kill passion at birth – clearing Cassanovas from boudoirs like moths from camphor-balled wardrobes. We all dreaded wet washdays, as in the evenings we had to compete with steaming clothes-horses for a place by the fireside.

Bodies also needed their weekly laundering, but none of the present-day luxury was to be enjoyed on bath nights at Newbound Mill. The same copper was used for heating the bathwater as for the clothes, the tin bath being unhooked from its stowage on the wash-house wall and set before the (hopefully) warm kitchen fire. The bath was of a size which comfortably allowed stretching of an eleven-year-old's legs, though for adults bathing must have been a rather crouched-up operation. Rudimentary calculations would have shown that the ratio of bath volume to below-waist volume of certain members of the family was such as to make overfilling a likely hazard; thus tidal waves which swamped the kitchen hearthrug were not infrequent.

Plans for segregating the sexes and age-groups on bath-nights were far from perfect, and more than once I was subjected to intrusive breaches of sexual etiquette. A few years earlier such niceties would not have worried me unduly, but by then I had reached an age when, for lack of comparison, I was unsure whether the sight of my dawning manhood would engender admiration or derision. All of this

lead me into the practice of a hurried soaping followed by a quick leap out and furtive towelling-down, in case I was discovered naked either by someone blundering in or by some Peeping Tom (or Thomasina). I did not like bath-nights.

For the house itself, cleansing time came at far less frequent intervals, as spring-cleaning was in fact carried out during that season only. This task occupied a considerable time and was carried out room by room, with great zeal. The part I detested most was carpet beating, for even rumours of vacuum cleaners had scarcely reached our neck of the woods. First came a laborious moving of furniture and dragging out of the unwieldy, corpse-like roll into the garden. Here, with heaves, grunts and muttered profanities it would be draped over a wall while hell was beaten out of it by we boy-slaves, using broom handles. A naive newcomer might imagine that six of the best would be enough to complete the job, but a seemingly inexhaustible supply of dust was released as by a conjuror from some concealed pocket. Good humour would finally be restored, for as the dust cleared Philip and I would burst into laughter at the sight of each other's coon-like eyes staring from sweaty, chocolate coloured faces.

As cleaning moved from room to room and corner to corner, spiders grown fat on easy living would flee uplifted brooms and probing feather dusters to find new homes for another year. One room would be selected each year for complete refurbishing, its ceiling being whitewashed and walls either colour-washed or re-papered, according to status. To me whitewashing meant smarting, bloodshot eyes, for I never got the hang of avoiding those blinding, alkaline drips and splashes.

All cupboards, drawers, wardrobes etc. would be turned out and inspected for things no longer required. This invariably produced a variety of unexpected bonuses.

Misplaced items would be found and treasured knick-knacks rediscovered. Hilda might be rewarded by some garment which had fallen out of favour with Mother, and I was sure to get some emptied tins and bottles from the store cupboard, for I could always find a use for them in my games and schemes. Sometimes guilty little secrets were uncovered, though only the silent culprit would know the full story behind the evidence of a half-sucked sweet or charred piece of brown paper.

Sweeping the chimney was an event which I always looked forward to, as it packed mild excitement into a short time, as opposed to the drawn-out bore of spring-cleaning. However, Father did not see it that way, and as this was a thoroughly dirty job and quite extraneous to the farmwork in hand, he would use any excuse to put it off. One delaying tactic was to use an 'Imp', a three-inch cube of some patent preparation designed to be placed in a red-hot fire, whence the powerful fumes so produced were claimed to dissipate the soot with ease. Certainly the eye-catching wrapper gave confidence, with a grinning imp apparently exulting in his magic powers. In the event, the results would fall somewhat short of the expectations aroused, and Father would be forced into naming a date for chimney sweeping. This was quite an event, all furniture etc. being covered with dust-sheets the night before, and an early start decreed. With sacking stretched across the chimney to contain the falling soot, rod after was screwed together as the brush was juggled higher and higher up the soot-caked chimney. My job was to stand outside and signal when the brush was sighted, and what a thrill it was to see it emerge from the chimney-pot with a few triumphant bobbings up and down. Anti-climax followed as Father packed up the brush gear and cleared up the mess, looking self-consciously comical as though he had blackened his face to try and raise a laugh. At least the soot was said to be useful for the garden or even cleaning the teeth, though I must confess to no experience of the former attribute nor any taste for the latter.

Brimstone-and-treacle day was another family occasion, when everyone lined up for a spoonful of that health-giving concoction, said to purify the blood. This was one of a number of stock medicines and nostrums kept in a special cupboard, as in those pre-NHS days falling sick could be a costly business. By the sound of their names, some of the medicaments could have come straight from the bow-fronted windows of an early Victorian apothecary's shop: paregoric, sweet nitre, tincture of rhubarb, liquorice root and a host of others. Each carried its reputation as a preventative, palliative or curative – cod-liver oil as a general body-builder, oil of cloves for toothache, or syrup of figs for constipation.

Although a range of branded items was stocked such as Friar's Balsam, Scott's Emulsion and Beecham's Pills, relief was often sought in more homely remedies; we would be plied with onion gruel, scorched with bread poultices, plastered with goose grease and then fortified with beef tea when on the mend. Granny remedies abounded, so in between drinking cups of nettle tea we would have our styes rubbed with gold rings, the laundry blue-bag applied to our wasp stings, and minor bleedings staunched by squirts from puff-balls. This latter item (a kind of fungus) seemed like something from a witch's bag of tricks, its wizened, spore-filled pouch being allotted a special place on the mantlepiece.

There being no specific against the swing of Father Time's scythe, death eventually claims us all, so one day found my parents thirty miles away at my maternal grandmother's funeral. By chance, all the rest of the family were away that evening also, which left me alone in the farmhouse after nightfall. In her Victorian widow's weeds and bonnet, grandmother Elliott had been a dour-looking, forbidding old lady, and had been found lying dead in her room with her stick lying by her side. Normal enough as that may sound, nevertheless those circumstances preyed on my imagination, so with Jack the dog for company I played with my model steam-engine in the kitchen, to occupy my mind until someone came home.

Suddenly terror struck in that lonely house: from the living-room came a thud and clatter – it must be She, re-enacting her death for my benefit! I fled terrified into the open, racing into the night across yard and field with Jack at my heels. After some two hundred yards an excruciating pain burst through to my brain, forcing me to drop the cause – my boiling-hot steam-engine which I had grabbed at the outset of panic. For a good hour I wandered in the cold and dark, desperate to get relief for my open wound but dreading to re-enter the house, till finally my parents arrived back. The scar disappeared from my hand years ago, but a trace still lingers in the mind.

To return to more agreeable things, what pleasanter occupation could be imagined than making butter? In actual fact, this soft-sounding job entailed a fair amount of work. Milk from the humble cows was first put through a cooler where it cascaded down over a series of fins, and then poured into a separator. This is where I came in, providing the motive power for gradually revving-up the flywheel to a speed where the cream was separated from the milk by centrifugal force. Cream from that whirling-dervish was transferred to a ten-gallon butter churn, and here again my puny fraction of one horsepower was used to keep the wooden barrel turning end-over-end via the handle. A steady rate had to be maintained until the smooth swishing changed to a more choppy feel and sound, which together with blobs sticking to a small inspection window announced that the butter was made. A thunderstorm in the offing would prolong the operation to a point where my aching arms longed for a rest, but even a short break meant a rapid relapse of the cream to its normal state, so it was a case of press on or risk Mother's wrath.

If my churning was successful I would be rewarded with a refreshing drink of buttermilk, much lauded also for its properties as a beauty aid. Of course the very name rolls so smoothly from the tongue that a latter-day song writer coined the phrase 'buttermilk sky', and some shrewd paint-sales promoter has named a particular shade after it. Most of our butter was sold, after being made up into pound or half-pound slabs, each patted into shape and imprinted with the Draycott logo of an ear of wheat. Finally the butter would be packed in a large, butcher's-type basket, and Mother would deliver it on foot, gathering news on the way from her customers all around the area.

Cream cheese was another milk by-product made at home, but the mainstay varieties such as cheddar and stilton were purchased in bulk on Market Day – an occasion worthy both of capital letters and a page or two of its own. It was as much a social event as a buying and selling time, so a little smartening-up was called for, Father putting on polished black leggings and wearing a collar and tie. When possible I might go as well, savouring the coming adventure during the half-hour's journey by trap to Mansfield or Chesterfield. Of the two places I favoured the latter, intrigued by the story that its church spire appeared crooked from wherever viewed, and never able to prove otherwise.

Father and I would part company for much of the time, and I thrilled to moving around on my own amid the jostle of people with its background of raised voices, animal lowings, bleatings and squealings, and the auctioneer's patter. This was a totally different world from Newbound Mill Farm – an exciting place where anything could happen.

Standing by the auction ring I studied the variety of weatherbeaten faces whose owners leant over the rails. With

wise-looking glances, prods and words with companions, they gave the impression of being able to value a beast to the last penny. I fell to wondering if I might be admitted to this sophisticated club where bids were made by the simple raising of a finger or mere winks and nods. After checking my meagre resources I moved over to where the lesser-fry of the livestock world were being auctioned, such as goats and rabbits. Waiting only a few minutes to get the hang of things, I entered the bidding. To my astonished delight, my first nod brought a sharp rap from the auctioneer's hammer, and after handing over ninepence I was the new and rightful owner of what appeared to be an equally excited ferret. Father would be proud of my astuteness at getting such a bargain!

In the event, Father was not impressed, being preoccupied with his own bargain carried under his arm – a complete stilton cheese. He had bid for this after first checking it in the traditional way, piercing the rind with his narrow, tubular sampler so as to withdraw a piece for tasting. This procedure struck me as open to abuse, for what was to stop anyone doing the rounds of all the cheeses on display, thus gaining a sizeable free snack.

On our way home we might have an extra passenger in the light cart, the face of calf, sheep or pig peering up through the rope-netting cover, wondering what this unexpected journey might lead to. Father would generally be in good spirits, the pleasure of his day out being heightened by a glass or two of beer, though in no way could he be called a drinking man. An extra drink over the clinching of a deal or whatever would make him pleasantly merry, but the mood would be spoilt on our arrival home, as Mother's rather straightforward views frowned on such wayward and dissolute goings-on – and in front of the boy as well!

Mother's strict religious upbringing also flavoured our Sundays, which were pleasant enough in some ways though not renowned for jollity of any kind. Sunday-best was the order of the day, even Mother's dainty apron at mealtimes signalling that something was different. To we semi-converts of the family, those meals were probably the best part of the day, as we could rely on a range of well-established favourites being served up. There could be roast beef and yorkshire pudding for dinner at midday, which in season would be accompanied by appetising new potatoes and peas fresh from the garden, shelled by me while sitting in the sun on the kitchen doorstep. That solid stone slab was often used by Father for sharpening the carving knife before attacking the joint. When I said midday I meant just that, for Mother was a stickler for the most rigid punctuality at meal-times, and woe betide any would-be offender.

Tea-time (4 o'clock sharp!) brought treats like delicious cream trifles and scrumptious sponge cakes, while supper often spelt the tastiest of rabbit pies with nutmeg-sprinkled egg custard to follow. Of course all of this had to be paid for by some form of penance, so late evening would find us sitting quietly in the 'best room', adopting sanctimonious expressions while Mother purged us of our week's sins by renderings from her standard hymnal – Sankey. And so to bed.

As Christmas approached each year, a date would be set for killing the pig. Squeamishness and a regard for your feelings prevents me from recounting the details of that animal's sad demise, so let me move on to the stage where it has been dismembered into manageable portions. Further processing of those parts into all the by-products associated with pig-killing was supervised by Mother's cousin Fanny from Wymeswold, who would duly arrive and take up residence for a few days. She was a pleasant woman, radiating cheerful efficiency and holding our attention both by her skills and her amusing small-talk.

We were at cousin Fanny's command as she called for mincing-machine, bowl, knife or chopping board, instructing this one to rub herbs and that one to peel onions, while walking around to check that everything was progressing according to her master plan.

The operation employed most of us and took up both kitchen and living-room, the heat and savoury odours from the two ovens intermingling through the open doorway between. By the end of the first day every available space on tables, dresser and windowsills was taken up with dishes of pork scratchings, collared head, sausages and the like, and meals had to be eaten in a room at the end of the passage.

One result of these activities was the correction of my sister Hilda's belief that sausages came ready-made from pigs, which led to my speculation as to what gave rise to that notion. The mind boggles at the sheer details of the possibilities, the most bizarre evoking a picture of a semi-robotic animal, with swill being poured in at one end and pork bangers emerging in a string from the other. Only Heath Robinson could have done justice to an illustration of such a contraption.

The last item in the programme was making the pork pies, two or three dozen of them being lined up on trays ready for transporting to Pleasley for baking. They were taken there by horse and trap, and as soon as fetched back would be topped-up with savoury stock through a funnel, while still warm. I can still taste the jelly and flaky fat pastry of those pies, and have never found anything to match the homely products of genial cousin Fanny.

After dispatching presents of pies etc. to all and sundry, and with legs of ham and flitches of bacon hung from stout hooks on the kitchen beams, we were ready for the next exciting event – Christmas.

A foretaste of Christmas Day came each year from our village school at Teversal, where closing day brought the handing-out of presents from the tree, each one (as far as possible) being as personally requested a week or so beforehand. This ceremony was performed by Lady Carnarvon whose husband died in 1923, reputedly a victim of the Tutankhamen's tomb curse, following which his widow had moved into the manor house at Teversal.

It was during those years that my faith in the actual existence of Santa Claus was gradually undermined and destroyed, but I do not associate that with any real diminuition in the joys of anticipation. That old trickster's arrival was preceded by the usual build-up of holly gathering, mince-pie making and furtive behaviour until finally and unbelievably Christmas Eve was actually upon us. The sound of a brass band playing 'While Shepherds Watched' still sends a shiver down my spine, recalling that devoted Salvation Army group who took the trouble to trudge round those scattered country homesteads.

Santa Claus or not, the most sleepless Christmas Eve vigil never seemed to reveal the precise moment when those bulging stockings were actually hung from the bedrail, and morning light would find Philip and I tearing the wrappings off clockwork motor-cyclist, toy gramophone, chemistry outfit or Boy's Annual, until there was nothing more to discover but the old favourites in the stocking toes – oranges, chocolate pennies, and monkey-nuts. That Christmas morning atmosphere was as though a crisis had been resolved, with everyone relieved at the outcome and exuding geniality.

Throughout the morning we played on table, chairs or hearthrug with our exciting new possessions, to a background of cheerful bustling as preparations for the Christmas dinner got under way. That meal was the most happy of family occasions, with Mother eagerly watching to see who found the silver threepenny-bits concealed in the plum pudding during mixing. I remember one occasion when she ensured that farm-hand Frank in the kitchen was not left out by secretly inserting a coin in his pudding. There being no response, she took through a second helping with another threepenny-bit in, but Frank's healthy appetite precluded such niceties as thorough chewing, so both coins slipped undetected into the labyrinth of his digestive system.

In the afternoon and evening, parlour games would be played such as Consequences, I Spy, and sticking on the donkey's tail while blindfolded. At dusk we would sit for a time with only the firelight and candles on the Christmas tree to strike frosty sparks of light from glitter-dust and tinsel. It was something approaching magic.

The day would end with us sitting in the semi-darkness while Mother lit the two candles in their hinged brackets on the piano, straining to read the music as she played and sang the old carols. We would join in with the words of *Once in Royal David's City, Christians Awake* and *Hark the Herald Angels Sing,* watching the candlelight and her face reflected in the polished dark wood of the piano. With the bass-note strings still vibrating from the last chord, the piano-stool lid would be closed on the music sheets: it was all over for another year.

5

FAVOURITE BITS AND PIECES

Our reasons for becoming attached to particular props as we play our part on Life's stage are often obvious, sometimes quite obscure. I have picked up a number of such items while poking around in Memory's attic, and propose to dust them down for a short re-acquaintance. Like all things found in a lumber-room, they are a fairly random lot, so I can promise only a minimum of continuity, but here goes.

In an attempt to present my list logically, I will start early in the day by returning to the subject of lighting the fire. Now disappointing as a failure to achieve a light-up was, nevertheless there could be a bonus, for if the supply of dried kindling sticks had been exhausted in the attempt I could call on the Witch. This lady was related to the chimney-sweeping Imp I mentioned earlier, being manufactured by the same company; she was of course a packaged fire-lighting preparation sold under that name. Like the Imp, she was enclosed in a striking wrapper bearing her picture, though I would say she was rather better at her job than he was at his own. The grinning hag was shown astride her broomstick, emerging exultant from a sea of flames. After dwelling for a while on that captivating picture, I would open the package and crumble the Witch's body among the reluctant coals, and then apply a match. In retrospect I am inclined to attribute her success not so much to fire and brimstone as to compressed sawdust and paraffin.

There is not far to look for my next friend – the poker. The temptation to lift that simple rod of iron when seated by the fire was virtually irresistible, though I was not alone in that failing. However, being the junior member of the family, to pick up the poker when others were present risked shouts such as "Put that poker down!" or "Here, let me do that!" Hundreds of poking-hours had thinned down the end, and attempts to straighten it by levering between the grate bars when red hot had introduced even more kinks. This was a pity as it made a useful tool for boring holes in wooden models, though the smoke produced was hard on the eyes. Once when in a particularly capricious mood, I singed the cat's fur with it, and when Mother rushed in at the smell of burning I suggested she check on the bread pudding in the oven. It was unwise to pick up the poker on entering the room as Philip left, for brotherly love was sometimes demonstrated by heating-up the handle for my benefit. On a pleasanter note, if a particular picture in the fire became boring, a single insertion of the poker could change the scene dramatically. Altogether, it was a useful standby for filling in a few empty moments, even if only to tap idly on the bars.

At first sight our breakfast table at Newbound Mill seemed an unlikely source for inspiration of any kind, yet one item there provided my passport for dreamy visits to the mystic East – the Camp Coffee bottle. I feel sure that a blown-up version of the label on that bottle would have been useful outside an army recruiting office, showing life in the forces at its most romantic. A moustached Guards officer sits nonchalantly on his stool outside a bell-tent, resplendent in his colourful uniform, while bending obsequiously over him is his turbanned Indian batman, proferring (what else but) his morning's Camp Coffee. That scene portrayed not only coffee essence but the very essence of the great British Raj itself. Surely the Himalayas were not far away, and probably that gallant officer was only taking a short break in between rescuing beleaguered hill forts from the attentions of cunning, fanatical tribesmen. I never tired of looking at that picture and indulging in fantasies of a dashing military life, but a glance through the window brought me back to earth; the nearest thing to a charger in sight was Gilbert munching his hay. It was time for school!

Talking of meal tables, Mother was a Mrs Beeton fan and so in turn was I. Not that I was in a position to put her advice into practice, but I loved reading it and looking at the pictures. My favourite place for wallowing in the admirable Isabella Beeton's works was in front of a blazing fire, lying on my stomach with head cupped in hands. There were of course two main subjects dealt with by Mrs Beeton, i.e. cookery and household management. The coloured pictures of ingredients and ready-to-eat dishes are amongst the most saliva-inducing ones I can call to mind, in spite of all the so-called advances made since Victorian times. It would take a whole range of superlatives to describe that gastronomic cornucopia. Brilliantly plumaged pheasants and long-bodied hares awaited Cook's attention, metallic-scaled trouts sulked on plates, downy peaches begged to be peeled, and pies invited knife and fork to break the crust and release their aromatic gravies. It was all too much when tea-time still lay a full hour ahead. In the household management section I found both the text and sketches equally intriguing. This was one of my early insights into a world completely alien to ours at home, where there were servants to do most of the real work, leaving their mistress with enough time to amuse herself with on points of etiquette and keeping the lower orders with their noses to the grindstone or knife-cleaner.

I imagine that Mrs Beeton would have approved of our mincing-machine, just as I took to it myself. No doubt in her case the under-kitchenmaid would have been called on to use it, but in our home this fell to my lot, chiefly because Mother had difficulty in coping with anything mechanical. Granted that in its dismantled state it resembled an aptitude test for a would-be treacle-mine engineer, yet after assembly and clamping to the kitchen table it appeared simple enough: you dropped nondescript lumps of flesh in at the top, turned the handle, and neat worm-cast-like extrusions emerged from the front. Flesh seemed the right word to use, as I always had a masochistic temptation to push my finger in – with visions of a Sweeney Todd and meat pie situation resulting. After its grisly stint of performing the first stage of our chewing for us, it was washed and packed away in its white linen shroud to await its next macabre assignment.

An item of kithenware which I would welcome back as a dear old friend was the horn cup, meaning a cup actually fashioned from some animal horn. It was dark brown, translucent, and roughly the shape and size of a half-pint tumbler. Now although for convenience I have just classed it as kitchenware, there is one (and one only) environment where it would truly feel at home – the harvest field. I suppose the cup's very simplicity was part of its charm, though here I must admit to being one of those who believe also that articles absorb atmosphere from their history and usage. That being so, what tales might that cup have told of harvests long ago, with Thomas Hardyesque characters acting out their loves and jealousies in a late-summer cornfield setting with scythes, sheaves and wicker meal-

baskets for props. Did some lusty young harvester once recline in the cool shade of an elm tree at bread-and-cheese time, casting lascivious glances over the rim of that cider-filled cup? And was the beautifully sun-tanned young object of his desire secretly aware of this, sitting relaxed with hands in lap as though merely gazing through the shimmer over the stubble? We shall never know. That cup was in fact only used by us at harvest time, though I would sometimes fetch it out merely to handle it and take imaginary gulps of some unspecified harvest-field brew. Perhaps I was the reincarnation of that lustful harvester, hoping to be re-united with my lost love through the magic of the cup.

One of my prized youthful possessions was a nugget of gold – or so I at first thought! Now I admit to being a fool, and that nugget was of course what is known as 'fool's gold'. To a mineralogist it was simply a fairly commonplace lump of iron pyrites, which I had obtained by some swapping transaction with a miner's son at school, but to me it was pirate treasure. That acquisition lead me to suggest the forming of two rival gangs at school, and as the initiator of the idea it was only natural that I should become one of the boss men. The pattern was that we would bury 'treasure' (coloured-glass gems, Victorian-button jewels etc.) and then make a map which our rivals had to try and steal. Of course we had to let them win in the end, so as to revel in the vicarious pleasure of them interpreting the map ('X' marks the spot, six paces north of an old wall then five towards a gorse bush) and then actually unearthing that untold wealth. For a long time I held back from using the ultimate treasure of the gold nugget in these dinner-time adventures, until finally I relented and buried it as part of a hoard. Sad to relate, something went wrong, so the nugget probably lies buried to this day, awaiting some metal-detector user to muse one day as to how a lump of shiny stuff came to be buried in a rusted Colman's Mustard tin along with a cheap brooch.

In my description of Christmas-time I mentioned that at Teversal school we could, within reason, name a particular toy to be waiting for us on the tree. One year I chose a clockwork submarine, and against my wildest expectations there it was under my arm as I ran home that end-of-term afternoon. A detailed check at home showed that, in appearance at least, it was all I had hoped for, with its sleek grey hull, conning-tower and general air of sinister menace. After a very short but satisfactory trip in the tin bath, I committed it to its sea trials in the mill-pond, starting with gentle turns on full rudder so that it circled near the stone harbour wall. Next came diving tests, with the vanes set for shallow submergings and re-surfacing. It was sheer joy! In my imagination I was in there at the periscope, a grim-faced U-boat commander, rapping out gutteral commands as the duelling scar on my cheek whitened with suppressed excitement. After possibly a glorious fortnight of these sort of manoeuvres, there came a day when I launched my submarine on a mission which took her across a long stretch of water. As always, after a short distance she dived, but uncharacteristically did not re-surface further on. A thorough search in safety was not possible: she was sunk without trace, lost with all hands – and within sight of Pondweed Point at that. The frogs continued to breast-stroke lazily across that sea, unaware that the flower of the Newbound underwater fleet lay in a watery grave, full fathom deep below them.

One present I received – a chemistry outfit – could have triggered off grave and paranoic doubts as to the parental motives, for around that time it was reported that some unfortunate lad had gone into orbit with his garden shed while re-discovering gunpowder. Although not disinterested in that branch of military science, I concentrated more on such harmless things as making nasty smells and a trick which apparently turned water into wine. I had just got into my stride with a tube of liquid and crystals which merely confirmed weather conditions already apparent by glancing out of the window and had achieved notoriety at school with an obnoxious smoke bomb, when my parents had their doubts. Following suspicions as to how a patch of the cat's fur had turned green, they scanned the label of that box of tricks and found a small-print caveat of "Suitable only for boys of fifteen and over." My promising career as a future Nobel Prize winner was at an end.

More compatible with my age was a toy which I bought during a short family holiday at the seaside. It was a tin frog, more endearing than the chemistry outfit but not nearly so versatile, for it had only one trick in its repertoire – it jumped. As an inventor of sorts myself, I give full marks to the frog's designer for the effective simplicity of its leaping device. A short leaf-spring on the underside was pressed into a recessed lump of cobbler's wax, the termination of adhesion resulting in a flick of the spring – and presto! The jump was delayed by a matter of seconds or minutes, according to the force applied when pressing the spring into the wax, which permitted little pranks to be played. For example, an unsuspecting victim might be invited to admire the frog's lifelike qualities, with a guaranteed startling result. All good clean fun, but on the last morning of our stay in the Skegness boarding-house the frog spoiled his record for reasonable behaviour. At breakfast time I placed him on the table after setting the spring with around a minute's delay, but the family had grown accustomed to him and took no notice. Suddenly, commotion! The frog had leapt clean into the sugar basin on the next table, showering sticky grains into the face of a sour-looking spinster bent over her cornflakes. After her frosty remark about unruly children, my shamefaced parents pocketed the wayward amphibian with muttered apologies. I cannot remember what happened to the lovable Froggo, but he was greatly missed.

One item found in the attic of our time-mellowed farmhouse when we first moved in would have excited many present-day antique dealers. How anyone could have left it behind is a mystery, for it was a copper powder flask for a muzzle-loading gun, with a beautiful design chased on the surface. I was allowed to use it as a plaything, as my parents obviously had no idea of its value to a collector of such things. It had a flip-open lid for filling with powder and a nozzle for inserting into the gun-muzzle. Like the horn cup, its pleasing though simple lines spoke of days when things were designed not only as functional objects but with an eye to their aesthetic appeal also. Sacrilegious as it may now seem, at that time my powder had to be dust, and my muzzle-loader a length of rusty tubing. The flask had obviously belonged to the place, and must have played its part in days of hunting over those same fields which Father now walked with his relatively modern double-barrelled twelve-bore. I always feel sorry for time-honoured things which are discarded when no longer of practical use, though where the flask actually ended up I know not. My worst fear is that it may eventually have gone unrecognised, progressing from rubbish tip to recycling into some modern junk or other.

I have never been a lover of what I would call 'pretty' ornaments – those over-sweet furbelows which sit on china cabinets awaiting praise from sycophantic visitors. To me, an ornament should have character, and that is exactly what my best-loved one had in abundance, though in another sense he was no ornament – he was a squashed-face pot bulldog! Apricot in colour, with his folds and creases picked out in sepia, he squatted foursquare on the bedroom dressing-table, guarding his young master against the would-be intruder. The fractional tilt of head, uplift of one ear-flap and quizzical look spelt hair-trigger vigilance, with swift action awaiting anyone who might 'try it on'. But towards me he showed a gentler nature, more in keeping with the smoothness of his glazed coat. It was comforting to know that whatever upsets or alienations arose in respect of others, he was always there if I needed sympathy. When I awoke in the night during illness, the nightlight would reveal him still sitting there faithfully, giving reassurance. He even aged along with me, for on leave from the RAF in 1942 I noticed a patina of fine lines under his glaze. Like most of my treasured things he eventually disappeared, for after Mother's death in 1969 I could find no trace of him.

Mother hoarded buttons on a grand scale, for the capacious striped-linen bag kept in the dresser contained not just hundreds but literally several thousands of them. The reason was easy to see, for not only had she obviously inherited many of them from two or three generations back, but also she never consigned a garment to rag-bag, rag-man or hearthrug making without first cutting off the buttons, buckles, hooks-and-eyes or other fasteners. The result was an Aladdin's cave of buttonery – a treasury of sartorial gewgaws. I had countless hours of amusement with the contents of the button-bag, as there were several games which could be played. Firstly, I could act the miser, dipping my hands in and letting the wealth trickle through my fingers. Then there was matching-up, challenging myself to find the complete set of a particular button. Arranging by shape or colour was another diversion, but as satisfying as anything was simple browsing, sifting through the jumbled pile to admire here the iridescence of a pearl button or there the ornateness of a Victorian one. That enchanting selection formed the source for most of my gang-warfare treasures, and happily odd items still survive in my wife's sewing box.

In my house today hangs a fairly crude oil painting which nevertheless is totally irreplaceable, for it shows my maternal great-grandmother outside her single-storey thatched cottage, with a couple of hens pecking around in the foreground. It forms a simple but direct link with my forebears, and as a boy I would sometimes study it closely in attempts to discern the details of that never-met old lady's features. No such luck, as the past tantalisingly withheld those secrets in a few anonymous blobs of paint. I wonder does she ever come back to look herself?

Our past-its-best Regency desk (or davenport in antique-trade parlance) hinted at better times and grander places than the living-room of a 20th-century tenant farmer. Pull out a drawer or hinge down the inlaid rosewood writing-top and a hotch-potch of items would be revealed, quite unlike those which probably graced it when Queen Victoria was still a child. No invoices in copperplate handwriting listing quails and guinea-fowl, but bloodstained butcher's bills for tripe and liver; woodbine packets instead of dainty snuff-boxes; postcards from Mablethorpe rather than scented letters from Bath, and so on. Stuffed in the pigeon-holes was a miscellany of corn samples, books of stamps, kidney-bean seeds, sealing-wax, Swan ink, rubber bands and knotted garter-elastic. It was a pleasure to use, though opening it out of mere curiosity could bring cross-examination as to the reason. A stealthy approach for a quick rummage-through was risky, as like anything in the house with doors, lids, drawers, steps or the like, it could betray the guilty party with its unique signature of clicks, creaks or squeaks. Sadly, through neglect in later life, the desk fell a victim to woodworm and was destroyed.

Of the same general vintage as our desk was the three-legged games table, its round top having a chessboard inlaid in light and dark woods. It usually served as a pedestal for the aspidistra, but fortunately there were times when that archetypal symbol of 1920's tedium was removed so that the table could be put to its proper use. At that time none of us were chess players, so draughts was the game. Philip was normally my opponent, but I preferred uncle Tom, who loved to play at cards, dominoes or draughts on his frequent visits. He did not rub-in his victories like Philip was inclined to do, and also was generally in a pleasant mood as he pulled contentedly on his pipe. His regular puffs of Bruno hung around us in perfumed clouds, and this appreciation of the good life was further evidenced by the glass of Mansfield Ale perched at his elbow on the table's edge. Like the desk, years later the table legs succumbed to woodworm, though I managed to rescue the top. It is uncle Tom I remember whenever I look at that chessboard, chuckling as he hopped over three of my draughts in one move.

The final three of my favourite things all concern oil lamps, starting with the paraffin can used to fill them. This may sound the unlikeliest of things to form the object of any attachment, but it all centred around its shape. The combination of its conical top, its spout, cap and handle gave it the appearance of some exotic bird, probably from the depths of a South American rain forest – say a quetzal for example. I could imagine it in a remote clearing, performing a bizarre courtship ritual. I loved also the slenderness of the stream of paraffin from that dainty beak when I filled the lamps. Over-fanciful? Maybe, but then what harm is there in such boyish imaginings?

Hurricane-lamps were amongst those filled from that paraffin can, and were in use virtually week in, week out. Again, these were things for which I had a genuine affection, and I cannot visualise life on the farm without them. They gained character in my eyes from their trademark of a bat with outspread wings, moulded into the lamp-glass. As they hung in the cowshed at milking-time on warm evenings, moths would be attracted to fling themselves softly at the glass, in doomed attempts to get closer to the flame inside. On dark winter nights, those pools of mellow light moving around farmyard or field brought a homely feeling and sense

of security. Incidentally, their name was well-deserved, for it was practically unknown for them to be blown out, even by the strongest winds.

Finally among my loved bits and pieces comes the Kelly lamp. For the uninitiated, this was a miniature brass oil lamp, used mainly where only a low light was needed and where safety was important. It had a weighted, rounded base, making it impossible to knock over. Its refusal to lie down lead me into hours of trying to defeat its self-righting capabilities. I would describe its waking-hours character as jolly and tolerant, whilst through the night it changed to a quiet, dependable friendliness. Normally it was only used in our bedroom when one of us was unwell, but I never gave up trying to appropriate it at other times.

And that seems a suitable note on which to put this chapter to bed.

6

DRESSED IN COUNTRY STYLE

Questions of fashion or style in clothing seemed to leave us fairly untouched at Newbound Mill. They could scarcely have been uppermost in my father's mind, and even if Mother had been so-minded there was not enough money in the family coffers to indulge in such vanities. In any case, the tenant-farming fraternity and country folk in general were not exactly trying to outdo one another in this respect. As for we children, a school community mixture of miners' and country villagers' children did not produce any real problems as to how we were dressed. Granted Hilda was just about to experience the normal young girl's preoccupation with clothing, but fortunately she had her talent for dressmaking as an outlet.

Our men's working dress was so predictable as to constitute almost a 'Land Army' uniform – corduroy trousers, loose jacket, collarless white shirt with stripes, hobnailed boots and cloth cap, not forgetting the red spotted handkerchief. Mess kit donned for smarter occasions such as market days consisted of cavalry-style breeches, a better-fitting jacket, collar and tie, trilby hat and polished leggings (black or brown, according to your regiment). A watch-chain looped across the waistcoat was *de rigeur*, its quality lending status, as did little extras like a breast-pocket triangle of white handkerchief, a flower buttonhole and neatly trimmed moustache.

Wide-bottomed 'Oxford bags' were the style of trousers worn by trendy young men, while the ridiculous, ballooning knickerbockers known as 'plus fours' were not confined to golfers but came to be associated with social climbers and snob-value clothing. Young mashers out to impress the girls wore smart jackets, waistcoats and trousers, spats buttoned over shoes, and either a bowler or straw-boater according to the season. Cane in hand, they would accost their quarry with a raising of headgear and opening gambits such as "Does your mother know you're out?" You may ask what all this has to do with country-style clothing, the answer being nothing directly, but it does give the background to other lifestyles as glimpsed through visitors, gossip or occasional trips to nearby towns.

For Philip and I, school clothing meant short trousers (generally of corduroy), jersey, collar and tie, stout boots and school cap. Many of the children at Teversal school, especially those from miners' families, were far less fortunate, as inadequate and often dirty clothing was all too common. Some boys and girls even wore jerseys or pathetically-thin dresses next to the skin, most garments being in need of mending. Even stockings or socks were a luxury for some, and decent footwear was a rarity also.

Boys are of course not exactly noted for respecting the conventions, and I can quote an example of this involving clothing. Having been forcibly retired to bed one hot summer night, though not nearly ready for sleep, I cast around for some way of passing the time. Catapults were in vogue, so I decided to improvise one by taking the braces from my trousers and anchoring them to the bedrails. A great time was had for a while, setting up targets on the dressing table and using whatever came to hand as missiles. All good things come to an end, in this case when Mother crept up the stairs to investigate. The fun did not cease entirely, for at least she seemed to enjoy the spanking she administered.

Clothing knick-knacks and fripperies were not exactly big business for lads of my age, as the use of such adjuncts to try and catch the eyes of the girls lay a few years ahead. There were however two items which could add a little distinction to our turnout, namely fancy belts and tiepins. Although braces were our mainstay to prevent us being caught literally with our trousers down belts were used on occasion, and one given to Philip particularly excited my envy. It was of the snake-clasp variety, and I longed to own one myself, with its jaunty coloured strikes and that S-shaped silver serpent. The best I could achieve in the way of rivalry was to flaunt my diamond tiepin, though some unbelievers alleged that the stone was only made of glass.

Our Sunday-best suits were of grey flannel, and not to be worn at any other time except similar high days or holidays. That did not worry us, as in any case the fear of dirtying or tearing them made the experience akin to wearing a straitjacket. There was a part-answer to this problem around that time, for I remember wearing a celluloid collar which could be wiped clean – handy both for mums and guilt-ridden jam stealers alike.

Like most country women of her age, Mother was inclined

to resist change by clinging to the styles of her earlier years. Thus her clothes tended to be darker, skirts a shade longer and hat brims wider than her 'townie' counterparts. Part of her best outfit for visiting was some animal fur (I forget which) complete with the small head. That fashion would be condemned by animal lovers today, but was commonplace enough at the time. For as long as I can remember, there was a practice which Mother followed religiously every day: she would always change into something brighter before sitting down to tea.

Sister Hilda, although not in a position to fully enter the world of the 1920s Clara Bow-type flappers, did at least get round to wearing a cloche hat, and probably copied them in other ways which I don't remember. The giddy life of those young women, Charlestoning away the time in short, fringed dresses, long necklaces swinging against their Oxford-bagged male escorts, must have seemed very attractive to the average young girl.

As a young boy, I found the terminology of women's clothing to have a mystique which set it quite apart from that of a mere male. I speak in particular of their upper underclothing (if you see what I mean), as from the girl-talk between Mother and Hilda I gathered that there was some complexity about it. Apparently they were not content with a simple vest, for I heard talk of shimmies, camisoles, corsets, stays, liberty-bodices and combinations. Even lower down, instead of plain trousers they had drawers, bloomers or cami-knickers. To show more than a passing interest in such garments should they accidentally be left in view would result in a quick whisk-away, presumably as items unsuitable to be seen by a growing lad. Perhaps when older I would be the subject of an initiation rite and led into a taboo room where all would be revealed.

We young males may not have fully understood the use for which women's stays were designed, but we did find an excellent use for the springs which they contained. These springs formed the trigger-cum-ejector for powering toy pistols which we made, the barrels being the hollow stems of cow-parsley whilst the bullets were hawthorn berries. Our supply of these springs came from rubbish heaps where discarded stays were to be found in abundance (the beginnings of Women's Lib?).

At the risk of appearing obsessed with the topic, I must recount one more memory which I later discovered was connected with women's stays. When abroad in Pleasley or Mansfield I was puzzled by plaques on several houses apparently advertising the services of a 'Spiral corsetiere'. I could get no satisfactory explanation from our adults, who indeed seemed embarrassed by my questions. There seemed to be some connection with maturer women, as occasionally I would glimpse them entering or leaving, rather furtively, with a parcel. Did the plaques refer to a device, secret society or French dancing master? The houses seemed drab enough, but then what went off inside? (To be continued next decade).

With three adults and three children under the roof, I really don't know how Mother kept up with the repairs to all that clothing. Certainly much of her so-called spare time was spent at it, and often I had to break off from reading or whatever to thread her needle for her. There was much patching of working clothes, and in the case of Father's jackets it provided an excuse for airing one of Mother's stock jokes – a reference to Joseph's coat of many colours.

Clothes taken out of drawers or wardrobes generally smelt either of camphor moth-balls or lavender, the latter being from our own garden, the flower heads having been dried and sewn into cloth sachets. These were agreeable enough as background smells but rather sickly in concentration.

When finally discarded, many clothes ended up in a huge

DRESSED IN COUNTRY STYLE

rag-bag, to provide cleaning rags and patching material etc. To we children it was our wardrobe for dressing-up games, which for me sometimes included the dogs. (Cats proved difficult!). Those wretched animals seemed to get little fun out of it, sensing how ridiculous they looked. After all, what self-respecting hound wishes to be seen wearing a baby's sun-hat and rompers?

There seemed to be a dressmaking craze around that time, both Hilda's and Mother's weekly magazines invariably containing a free, paper dress-pattern. These were flimsy jigsaws of arms, shoulders, cuffs, collars and so on, begging for material to be cut, pinned and sewn into the finished product. This latter was depicted on the packet by Identikit young ladies, half turned to throw demure yet beguiling glances over their shoulders. Dressmaking evenings would result in table, chairs and floor being spread with patterns, and the following days carried a high risk of getting pins in stockinged feet or bottoms. Sometimes the first fitting would produce puzzlement, until it was discovered that an arm had been sewn on backwards, or the back apparently tailored to accommodate a baby camel. Reference to the picture was no help, the young lady merely offering a supercilious smile.

Except possibly for Hilda, hairdressing was carried out on a self-help basis, Hilda attending to Mother's homely coiffure, Father being our barber and Mother his own. This resulted in something less than tonsorial elegance, though personally I had yet to reach an age where such things mattered a great deal. The actual process of haircutting was always an ordeal for me, as Father had neither the expertise nor patience for the job. Try as I may, I never seemed to interpret correctly his instructions as to the positioning of my head. Things would end in him gripping me roughly, apparently intent on twisting my head to the limits of its capability. I believe much of the troubled stemmed from the fact that he often drew blood, so that I was given to anticipatory flinches and audible wincing, making life even more difficult for him. Father was not given to outright swearing, but I remember one haircutting session drawing from him the remark that he wished someone else would do the "lousy" job – an unfortunate choice of adjective in the circumstances.

We boys would use brillantine on our hair when togged up for special occasions. This could be either of the liquid or solid type, both resulting in Mother watching us closely to ensure that greasy heads were not leant against the backs of the easy chairs, sofa, or even the wallpaper. Social history experts will know that this hazard gave rise to the use of antimacassars, those protective covers for furniture fabrics which took their name from the hair-oil used by Victorian gentlemen. These embroidered coverlets were prized by Mother as part of the general decor; in my mind they tended to rank along with the aspidistra as marks of a parlour-type primness.

This was the era of a few odd hairstyles for women, like eton-crops and 'wireless coils' over each ear, and of course advertising had conditioned them into the belief that 'Friday night is Amami night'. On the other side of the coin, a few unfortunate young girls at our school did not enjoy any hairstyle at all, as following an inspection at school by the 'head nurse', they suffered the indignity of having most of their hair cut off.

Shaving was a grooming process much in the future for me, but I took pleasure in fiddling around with the equipment used by my father – all except for the cut-throat razor which was stowed away elsewhere. There was a combined bowl, soap-and-brush holder and adjustable two-sided mirror, one face being a magnifier. I suppose I looked on shaving as a manly activity, but had to obtain my satisfaction second-hand by studying Father when engaged in it. He seemed much better at it than cutting my hair, stretching the lathered skin of his throat, holding his nose aside and giving himself looks of appraisal as the greying stubble was transferred from face to blade to wad of newspaper. It appeared to be a satisfying experience, and I longed for the time when I too could enjoy it.

Shaving was also the time for moustache trimming. Father's moustache was a cross between the Charlie Chaplin and walrus styles, so did not require the waxing of those spikes which the more pompous males affected. This reminds me that one reputed recipe for young men having difficulty in growing a moustache was to rub in the green end of a goose-dropping. I incline to the view that this may have been on the recommendation of some rival-in-love, as any attempt to steal a kiss after applying that unsavoury ointment would certainly receive an unexplained rebuff – unexplained because in those days even his best girl-friend would not have told him why.

A walking-stick or cane gave the finishing touch to a man's turnout, particularly for his leisure hours. The wide variety available lent a touch of colour to any social get-together, and they could be personalised so that no two were exactly the same. My Father's stick for walking-out was elegantly slender, and remarkably flexible yet strong. The right-angled handle was made from a stag's antlers, with a hallmarked silver band below. Some of the stick handles were carved into amusing shapes such as human, animal or birds' heads. All told they were fascinating personal belongings, worthy of consideration today by anyone looking for some class of items to collect.

For the ladies, the range of adornments gave plenty of scope for completing their toilet, though Mother was rather conservative in this respect. She scorned any sort of facial make-up, but she loved her brooches. Some she wore had been handed down to her, but most had been bought by the family, as the present of a brooch was always well received by her. She would never wear earrings, bracelets or bangles, but was not averse to flower or cherry decorations on her straw hats, or hatpins with fancy heads. Bead necklaces were another of her favourites, and more than once a broken string would result in me undertaking a hands-and-knees search of floor, rugs, nooks and crannies, though seldom was a one-hundred percent match achieved when I restrung them. To be honest, I did not dislike this task, as throughout life I always responded to any form of challenge – even humble ones like finding lost beads!

Naturally Hilda's age and attitudes made her less constrained than Mother in the matter of female baubles and fripperies. Like most young girls, I suppose she was to some degree influenced by the (alleged) American way of life which the cinema often portrayed. I can still picture her tiny bottles of Parma violet perfume and attar of roses, though I suspect that the wafts therefrom owed more to synthetic chemistry than essential oils.

7

EARNING MY SATURDAY'S PENNY

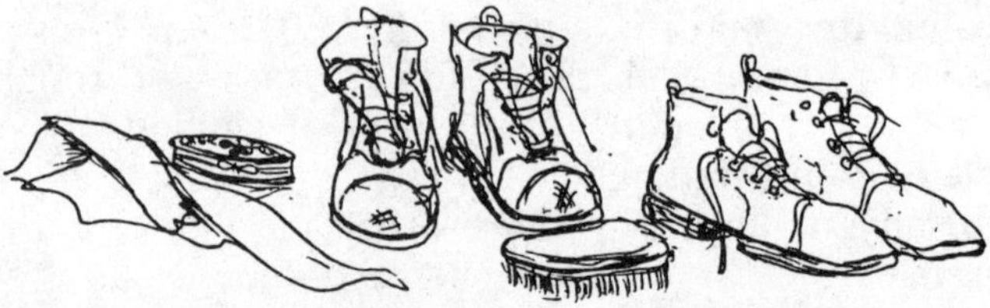

My parents' subscription to the Victorian virtues included a belief in the dignity of labour, which is a euphemism for "Get on with your work!" In my case it meant simply that if I expected to receive a penny or two each week for sweets, an extra comic or some other pandering to the flesh then I must earn it. Looking back, I consider this to have been a reasonable part of my upbringing but at the time it was often irksome, as usually I had some other interesting little ploy in mind. The various tasks I was given in this respect do not include work in the fields, as that constituted 'overtime' which I shall speak of elsewhere.

Many of my wage-earning chores were of a recurrent daily or weekly nature, so I soon became accustomed to the techniques and other ins-and-outs involved and the quality of work expected of me. A good example of this was my responsibility for ensuring that on each Saturday there was a supply of kindling sticks sufficient for firelighting throughout the week. Having assessed the existing stock of kindling (if any) by dividing into arbitrary-sized bundles, there was the question of where the remainder was to come from. With any luck the men would have left a suitable supply of sawn logs for splitting up, failing which a scour-around was necessary to find sufficient scraps from the farmyard or dead branches from trees and hedgerows. The first good swing of the axe during log-splitting revealed the wood's true character – compliant or obstinate, the former bringing straight-grained pleasure, the latter knotty problems.

Replenishment of the coal bucket kept by the fireside was sometimes my job, sometimes Philip's, but there was a period when he would pull rank as the elder whenever parental adjudication in the matter was not available. Annoyed, I laid my plan. There came a time when Philip once again smugly started to shovel onto the fire the results of my labour, though on this occasion I found it necessary to occupy myself elsewhere; within seconds a startled brother was taking refuge from a fusillade of flying stone from the blackened pebbles I had mixed with the slack!

Maintenance of our lighting often fell to me, but I did not find this too disagreeable as it brought its excuse for playing with fire. After topping-up the oil lamp with paraffin I would trim the wicks by removing first the charred layer and then any resultant ragged bits. A trial run came next, as any slight imperfections in the contour of the wick would be exaggerated by the flame, like a graph distorted in order to present some biassed political propaganda. Finally the brass body would be given a quick polish, at which stage I could take amusement in moving my head so as to produce gross 'hall of mirrors' reflections of my face.

Cleaning the candlesticks could be fun also. After removing the spent matchsticks and broken-off wick ends from the saucer-shaped base, the lava-like pools of wax were gouged out, providing the material for a few idle diversions of mine. The clean bits could be chewed – strange as that may sound! The taste was so bland as to verge on being sickly, but the texture was fascinating and the wax never clung to the teeth like toffee, and the lump never diminished. Changing of the wax to that texture could also be achieved by prolonged kneading between the fingers, when it could be drawn out into ropes like a showman making rock at a fairground. Alternatively I would mould it into shapes, like a witch fashioning images of some unsuspecting victim earmarked for the pin-sticking treatment. Once, acting on a suggestion from a boys' magazine, I made myself a candle-clock with coloured segments to mark each hour as burning progressed.

Next it was back to business, for there was a supply of spills to be made for lighting those oil lamps and candles, or for lighting Father's occasional Woodbine cigarette (Players if visitors were present!). The more-durable spills were made from soft, straight-grained wood, though a cheapjack variety consisted of strips of newspaper, tightly folded and creased. Each kind rested in a jam jar at one corner of the hearth next to the poker and fire-tongs.

Sometimes Mother would co-opt me into helping prepare the weekend dinners by giving me jobs where little could go wrong: picking the peas or kidney beans, cutting a cabbage or pulling a few sticks of rhubarb from the garden were all undemanding little obligations. Cutting the beans was slightly more difficult, as there seemed to be very narrow limits of acceptability regarding the thickness of those succulent, juicy slices. My regular job of peeling the potatoes was not over-welcome, as Mother was inclined to niggle over the odd eye or two left in. Very little escaped her inspections when she was wearing her head chef's hat. I did not mind being asked to do the pastry-cutting for mince pies, jam tarts and so on, as there was satisfaction in stamping out those crinkly-edged shapes, and virtually nothing to go wrong and invite criticism.

Leading off from the kitchen was a large room known as the coal-house, for the earth-floored far end was in fact used for that purpose. The nearer part was crudely tiled, and had a massive piece of furniture just recognisable under its stains, grime and scars as an old dresser. The top of this sturdy workhorse formed the bench for one of my Saturday Jobs which I detested most of all, for amongst my other roles I was Hotel Newbound's boot-black. The chief housemaid (Mother) would line up the week's quota on the bench-top and I was left to it.

In wet weather Newbound Mill and its surrounds were not exactly short of mud, and whilst the owners of that footwear may have given it perfunctory scrapings and brushings, there would invariably be congealed layers of Mother Earth to be removed somehow before tarting-up with blacking dare be attempted. I would stand looking at that row of boots and shoes with increasing gloom, generally unable for some minutes to make any sort of move. Should I start with the worst ones and get that over with, or would I feel better by gradually breaking myself in with the cleanest pairs? Finally it would sink in that there was no way out of it, and there was other work awaiting me as well.

The box of boot-cleaning gear was well equipped with items for every operation, the first required being a large, old-fashioned, notched and blunted dinner knife, with a yellowing bone handle. No doubt it had started life in some grand house, slicing its way through roast woodcock or nudging potatoes *a la maitre d'hotel* onto its companion fork, but now, in pathetically reduced circumstances, it must scrape the dried dirt off our footwear.

With the dirt gouged and brushed off to the point where most of the leather was visible, my spirits would lift at the prospect of applying the polish, the part which I did not mind at all. First there was the tin of Cherry Blossom polish to be admired, both the name and picture alone cheering me up. The standard method advised for prising off the lid always struck me as like using a sledgehammer to crack a nut, for into a groove must be inserted and twisted a penny – a whole week's wages! New, unopened tins brought the thrill of that first dip of the brush into the pristine, ebony surface of the blacking.

Polishing and buffing brought the process to the inspection stage, and Mother would re-don her chief housemaid's cap and cast an eagle eye over my handiwork while I stood guiltily to one side. Would she or would she not spot the slightly duller patches where blacking had been applied over stubborn layers of dirt? Right first time!

There was a miscellany of non-routine jobs around the house which cropped up from time to time, two of which Mother so dreaded that in no way could she have done them herself, so they were requested of me rather than ordered. It would be "Walter, would you mind . . . " or " . . . do you think you could . . . " – which put me in a commanding position for a change. I did not care for either of those jobs myself, but was determined to show what a brave and useful little lad I was after all. The one I loathed most was being asked to fetch something from the cellar, as it was dark, damp and scary, and above all the toad lived somewhere in there, not like the one resident in the garden, but the very Prince of Darkness himself. I would make a hesitant, tiptoed approach by candlelight, make a quick, snatch-squad grab at the article required and hare back up the steps into the real world of daylight. Phew!

The other distasteful job was checking the mousetraps in the attic bedrooms. There could be those unsprung but with the cheese gone (faulty setting or crafty mice), those unsprung with a morsel of stale cheese still intact (no mice, or only suspicious ones), or worst of all the sight of a trapped head with accusing dead eyes, guilty of nothing more than satisfying a natural appetite for something we ourselves enjoyed. I would then have the sad job of disposing of the little body, holding the trap at arm's length as I ran down the stairs and out across the yard to the manure heap. Re-setting the traps really was hazardous for me, and it took a few extremely painful trapped fingers before I learned the technique. I never fully conquered the feeling that in setting those traps I could be the executioner of creatures condemned without a trial.

A more humane service rendered by me as and when called on was watering the house plants, possessions which gave Mother lots of pleasure and which she treasured as though they formed some special collection. Personally I found many of them (though not all) dull beyond belief, yet often when visitors called they were admired, touched and had their potted histories (!) recited as though newly acquired from the South Seas via Captain Cook's *Discovery*. This one favoured being by a window, that one couldn't stand the cold, and the other one only flowered the week before every alternate Christmas. However, they had their uses for I discovered that one of them could easily be lifted clean out of its pot, small objects secreted underneath, then quickly dumped back in again.

Periodically the cutlery was cleaned (it was not grand enough to be called the silver), and fortunately this was normally a joint effort, two or three of us sitting at the kitchen table which was protected by old newspapers. As we rubbed away with Brasso-impregnated rags, we generally found plenty to chatter about, but should the conversation tend to flag then a random glance at the newspapers was bound to find some fresh topic – *Ben Hur* was due at the cinema, a man had been bound over for beating his wife, or the price of damsons had gone up again. The results of our elbow grease was a satisfying gleam on the table for a few days, but it was not unknown for a while to hear complaints about the mutton or porridge tasting of metal polish.

Another spit-and-polish job with which I helped now and then was window cleaning. It was not what I would call a regular job, for although Mother was particular enough over such matters we were scarcely in the stately homes business, nor were we overlooked by any Joneses with whom we wished to keep up. This is just as well, as otherwise they might have been rather startled on one occasion to see me apparently trying to make an end of it all via a bedroom window, with Mother clinging on desperately to either save or deter me from such an act! That would have belied the facts somewhat, the truth being that I had persuaded her to let me try out my patent rag-on-a-cranked-stick cleaner, while she acted as a sort of anchor-man. The idea was short-lived, but seemed a good one at the time.

A make-do-and-mend activity into which Mother tried to draw me was the question of buttons, and in fairness sewing on missing ones did eat into her time. She came up with the idea that the use of those new-fangled bachelor buttons might help a little, but as she seemed unable to cope with anything even remotely mechanical, she appointed me as her trials engineer. This proved to be one of those heroic failures, for by some miscalculation I positioned that first experimental button incorrectly on my Sunday-best flannel trousers. This seemed a trivial enough error, involving a straightforward removal and resiting of the button, but that innocent looking invention proved to have a one-track mind. It had been told to hold on at all costs, and true to the British tradition it did just that, with a bulldog-like tenacity which defied all attempts with pliers, screwdriver and hammer to remove it – or nearly. Suddenly it came off, complete with approximately one square-inch of flannel trouser. I was dismissed from my post as trials engineer.

Taking messages or running errands was mildly exciting and a welcome change from the same old faces and places. I would be handed sealed notes to take to this or that neighbour, sometimes returning with mysterious parcels, also tightly sealed. Mrs Smith down the lane always seemed to recognise quality, telling me what a nice lad I was and giving me sweets. One errand to the grocers left me with a puzzle which I did not solve until several years later. Apparently Mother was short of sugar for a baking session which she had planned, so I was dispatched the one-and-a-half miles to Pleasley. I walked up the hill, whistling and swiping off cow-parsley heads with strokes of the black oilcloth shopping bag I had been given. I then turned down the high street of this big mining village, eventually presenting myself at the counter of the grocer's shop and giving my order: "Two pounds of castrated sugar, please." The white-aproned male assistant paused, suppressed a giggle and said "Could you say that again please". I repeated my order and, obviously still amused, he turned away saying "I'll just get someone else to serve you". This seemed slightly odd to me, but it gave me the chance to stare around, taking in all the interesting looking packets, jars, tins and bottles on the shelves, and sacks standing on the worn, wooden floor. A second assistant appeared from behind the scenes and asked "Can I take your order sonny?", and my reply again caused the same amusement. What was so funny about sugar? Before I was eventually served, the shop looked like a Bateman cartoon, with several assistants lying semi-helpless on counter and sacks of flour as they laughed at 'The lad who asked for castrated sugar!' I felt both humiliated and puzzled, even more so when both of my parents succumbed to the same merriment when I told them my story. Mother's explanation that I had confused castor with granulated sugar still seemed no full excuse for all that hilarity. What a queer sense of humour adults had at times!

The dogs Jack and Gyp were put in my care for a wash and brush-up whenever deemed necessary. Both were reasonably placid, though between the two I could be surer of Gyp's behaviour, for she would submit to the treatment to the point of fawning, standing quietly as she was soaped down and flashing appealing sideways glances. Jack was of sterner stuff and proudly independent. His general demeanour indicated that whilst he admitted that I had my job to do, he would not agree that I had a licence to pull him around without due regard for his dignity. Should the limits of his patience be approached, he would give a warning growl, and fortunately I understood this dog-talk as clearly as I would if rebuked by my human elders.

Having diverted for a while to describe that variety of jobs which only arose spasmodically, I can now revert to the regular ones, though this time it concerns attending to the livestock rather than domestic work. I was in fact almost a full-time keeper to the hens and ducks, letting them out and feeding them in the morning, collecting their eggs in the late afternoon, closing their pens at dusk, and cleaning them out each weekend. In addition, I was normally either at or walking to and from school most of the day, so I was not exactly idle at any time.

Our quack-and-cackle community's day would start when I opened up the doors of their various residences, ranging from brick-built luxury to ramshackle wooden affairs. The hens would tumble out and leg it towards their feeding troughs like alcoholics at opening time. They would be followed by the ducks, also in a hurry, but waddling with a clumsy gait more suited to a quiet stroll. All and sundry knew that their breakfast would be waiting, normally grain but supplemented also by warm bran-mash on winter mornings. What a cacophony of squawks, cackles and quacks there would be; the hens would tuck into their steaming mash with gusto, while the ducks shovelled up greedy beakfuls of grain. On bitter winter mornings I would thaw out the ice on their drinking troughs, using a little of the hot water used for mixing the mash. After blowing on my own frozen nails it was time to leave them all to it and make my own way to Teversal school.

On my return from school my poultry-tending routine

would vary according to the season, as in winter Mother would already have collected the eggs while in summer it fell to my lot after tea. On the face of it that sounds a simple enough job, a quick check of each straw-lined nest-box. In practice, it meant searching haylofts, hedgerows, nettle-beds and a host of other hideouts over a wide area, for our hens were free-range in the true sense, with minds of their own. Advocates of the battery-hen system will of course argue that hens virtually have no minds, but such vested-interest nonsense comes from people who would be the first to shout if they were forced to eat bacon-and-egg pellets through prison cell bars all their life. Granted hens are positive imbeciles by human standards, but because they may mistake decoy pot eggs for the real thing, does that warrant us depriving them of their natural right to peck, scratch and cackle around field and farmyard at will?

Saturday mornings brought one of the jobs I disliked the most – cleaning out the hen-houses. With most of the hens out and around, it became a pattern for me to enter and sit on the lowest perch myself, head cupped in hands as I gloomily contemplated the task ahead. It brought me the same despondent feeling as did shoe cleaning, as there seemed no end to it. Sometimes I would have the company of an equally morose-looking hen, and this would bring a kind of therapy. I would turn to musing as to why she chose to be on her own while all her fellows were outside enjoying the good life. Was she unwell, or had she been sent to chicken-Coventry? She would eye me up in return, and sympathy seemed to flow between us till eventually I would feel better. I would then bestir myself to the job of scraping and forking together a mixture of hen dirt, straw and feathers, shovelling it onto the wheelbarrow drawn up by the door.

Wet weather could be either good or bad news in relation to hen-house cleaning, dependent largely on how many hens

had decided to stay indoors for a get-together rather than brave the elements. For me, the bigger the crowd the better, for I would then call in Father for a decision, and with any luck he would tell me not to turn them out, thus postponing my job. This brought sunshine to my heart, but should Mother have to deputise for Father, then the outlook was invariably 'continuing wet and gloomy'.

Now with hand on my heart I can truly say that, dimwits as sometimes they may seem, there are no creatures more lovable to me than hens and ducks; however, equally there can often be none more infuriating when it comes to putting them to bed. I say this on the basis of much experience, for closing and locking their pens against predatory foxes and humans was one of my nightly jobs. Winter nights brought little trouble in this respect but, like children, on pleasant spring or summer evenings they simply wanted to stay up late. Some of the old fogies could be bad enough, but the real problems came from headstrong teenagers and yellow thistledown-coated toddlers. Around dusk, I would hang around waiting for the last gawky young pullet to make up its mind, then as it entered the pen I would leap forward and slam the door to – generally to find the stupid bird had beaten me to it and run back out again! Occasionally one would be trapped by the neck, with an alarming flurry of feathers and strident screeching. I was never patient by nature, and ten minutes or so of this cat-and-mouse game would bring me to the verge of distraction. It would have started off mildly enough, as I edged forward with arms outstretched in a gentle, shepherding gesture, calling a quiet "chuck, chuck, chuck, there's a good bird"; sadly, matters would soon escalate till I was skidding around after a hysterical pullet, abusing it with words I had been warned never to use!

The broods of fluffy chicks could be just as frustrating. At twilight, although most of these little chirpers would be settling under their mother's fluffed-out downy skirt, there would generally be three or four wandering in and out through the vertical slats of their coop. The situation might be compared to a race-meeting starter's problems, the 'Off' being my quick push-across of the sliding door. Seldom could I achieve a first-time success, and the startled cheeping which resulted would cause Mother Hen to eye me with stern disapproval and warn me with angry cluckings, like some feathered matron from a Walt Disney cartoon.

I cannot truthfully remember the exact amount of my regular weekly 'wage' for those jobs at a particular age, though I believe that at one time it was threepence (1.25p), but traditionally it was always known as the Saturday's penny or ha'penny. Whatever the figure, the coins would be put in the ever-open mouth of my letterbox-style red moneybox until required. It seldom stayed in there for very long, the demand for cash being imperfectly matched by the supply; there was striped humbugs, acidic kali-suckers and mouth-filling gobstoppers to be bought, while from time to time the 'twopenny rushes' at Pleasley's cinema would be patronised, sitting in the 'flea pit' watching the macho exploits of cowboy Tom Mix. The good life!

8

BARNYARD, MILL AND FIELD

At Newbound Mill it was not a case of walking down the road or even just stepping across it to get to work: we were right in the middle of it all the time. Look out of the house windows to the north and you might spot Daisy, the senior cow, drinking from a stone trough in the stockyard which adjoined the house, with Gilbert, one of the three horses, watching her across the yard from his stable door. Cross the room to the opposite window and you could look south over the garden and roof of the old mill. Climb two floors up to my bedroom and there was a view from the only window at that end, eastwards across the fruit trees to where the mill stream flowed under the ancient stone bridge. Turn your back on that scene and walk the length of the house through the top bedrooms and you would be overlooking the main farmyard, with buildings clustered all around. It was indeed a farmstead in the true sense of the word.

That last yard just mentioned was reached merely by stepping outside the back door, which lay straight across the yard from the narrow main road. Approaching the house across the yard was not in fact achieved without first being vetted by Jack the house-dog. His sentry-box kennel was at the corner of the house, the length of his chain allowing him to patrol right across the threshold and challenge any stranger with a gruff "Friend or foe?" The various buildings around that large, open yard each had its own interest for one, so I propose to make an anticlockwise mental tour around them, re-living some of the sights, sounds and smells of those schoolboy years which now linger only in the form of fragmented memories.

Out of the back door and past the stockyard over the low wall to right led to the granary. This first-floor building lay over a barn and was entered from outside after climbing a flight of stone steps, worn hollow by generations of heavy farm-boots clattering up and down. Philip and I would dare one another to jump off the top of the steps onto the hard ground below, a foolish trick which was very hard on the feet and ankles. Naturally the granary was a favourite haunt of rats, and I recall Father calling on the services of a rat-catcher who duly arrived and impressed us all with his sales talk and highly technical-looking equipment. After telling us he had blocked up all their boltholes except one, he proceeded to pump into their network of runs what he claimed to be "the same gas as killed the soldiers in the trenches". We were warned to stand well clear of the lethal fumes and the expected outrush of such rodents as would try to escape. Disappointment followed, for not a single bewhiskered rascal emerged. Our Pied Piper left with the assurance that they must all have died at their posts, and possibly the till of some local pub rang to another tune that evening as he downed pints at Father's expense. The nuisance in our granary continued unabated.

The granary also fronted the road, from which it had a second access via a door high up in its stone wall. Here the farm waggons could draw up to discharge their loads direct, with no worry about parking on double yellow lines; there was very little chance of inconveniencing anyone else using the road, for even horse-drawn traffic other than our own carts was a rarity.

Leaving the granary and continuing round the yard led first past the low stone trough fed by the spring of beautiful drinking water which I mentioned in an earlier chapter. The constant noise of that running water was a feature of the yard, the very sound seeming to lend a coolness to drowsy summer afternoons.

Past a large five-barred gate and then a small hand-gate, each set between, large stone pillars, was the first of a right-angled range of outbuildings. Here was to be found such a variety of sacks, tools, drums and oddments of ironmongery etc. as defies even a broad classification. From stout nails driven into its delapidated walls hung forgotten oddments of harness, ropes and chains, festooned with dust-covered cobwebs. On entering, startled birds would make panicky flutterings among the rafters then suddenly swoop down through the open door and wheel swiftly up and away over the rooftop. On a crumbling windowsill lay a tattered seed catalogue, its half-opened pages thick with dust and bird droppings. Gyp, the collie bitch, would kneel by a pile of junk in the corner, her excited sniffs, pricked-up ears and wagging tail betraying the presence of some unseen mouse. This shed was set slightly apart from the remainder of the outbuildings both physically and in character, but I forget the distinguishing name by which it was known.

The neighbouring line of buildings lay alongside a cobbled

path, the first being a pair of stables where the two carthorses Prince and Darkie lived. At times these two stalwarts would stand with their heads poked out of the open top half of their doors, engaged in their own silent communications or surveying the general scene in the yard. Other times would find them tethered at their mangers, steadily munching their oats with a regular crunch of molars audible from way outside. Even a short look in at them could bring a sharp involuntary snatch of the head and smarting of eyes from the ammonia in their golden urine which trickled along the glazed-brick runnels. In a strange way, even the smells from these noble animals could not be called offensive. Their sideways glances as they became aware of my head peeping over the door or when they heard the click of the latch generally conveyed friendliness or plain nosyness; satisfied that they were not being fetched out for work or about to be groomed, their heads would reach up to pull another mouthful of hay from the rack above the manger.

Conveniently next door to the stables was the harness room. Outside here the horses would be prepared for the particular task ahead by selecting, putting on and adjusting the various straps, lines, buckles, hooks, chains and what-have-yous that go to make up this strange conglomeration of leather, brass and iron. I speak in these terms from a sense of inferiority bred by never having fully understood or been able to name all the parts of a set of harness. Certain bits were obvious even to a layman, as clearly there must be a collar with which to dress the animal and a pair of reins whereby to steer it, but at any suggestion that I should pry deeper into the secrets of that complex looking array, my mind would lie down and refuse to try and take it all in.

To my great chagrin Philip seemed to understand how the harness was all put together and worked, and possibly this was where the root of the trouble lay with me, knowing that

he was always one-up in this particular branch of know-how. Secretly I had a grudging admiration for his talents in harnessing a horse to a cart, trap or other farm vehicle; once when I had been told to hitch things together and gave Darkie the "Gee up!" command, after the first couple of paces forward the shafts dropped to his ankles, and the horse's lips seemed to curl back off his teeth in a sneer of contempt at my ludicrous bungling of a simple operation.

One of the most exciting farm buildings, for me at any rate, lay next to the harness room. We called it the engine-room, for when in active use its throbbing heart was a Lister engine which powered any one of three machines bolted to the floor: there was a small food-grinding mill, a cow-cake breaker and a chaff-cutter. Like many of its era, that engine would be very temperamental when called on to do a job of work, and possibly sensed that mechanical matters were not Father's strongest suit. After the initial procedures of priming and control setting Father would crank away with the detachable starting handle, a succession of grunts and wheezes from both parties often ending with a loud spit-back and flying handle. Father would leap around nursing a sprained thumb, mouthing his version of obscenities with "Dal the thing!" or "You mucky blighter!", but all to no avail, as the obstinate machine was impervious to cursing or putting the boot in alike – until it had worked the chip off its shoulder. In fairness, once started up it ran smoothly enough, the stored energy in its flywheel coping with any short bad spells, like a camel's hump during the lean times of desert crossings. The steady phut-phut and smoke-rings from the roof-mounted exhaust told of beans being ground, straw chopped into shreds or linseed-oil cow-cake broken into chewable little nuggets.

Next in the line of buildings lay the bin-room, so called because one wall of this animal grocer's shop was lined with huge wooden bins full of the flour-meal, bran, maize, ground peas and beans used for mixing up tasty dishes for the livestock. There were stock recipes for different animals and poultry – three scoops of this and one of that stirred into such-and-such a fraction of a bucketful of water, to make pigs' soup, hens' porridge or cows' dumplings, hot or cold according to the time of day or season. The recipes were pencilled crudely on the whitewashed wall above the bins – "Fowls (winter) – ½ barley, 2 wheat", "Prince – no beans" etc. etc. There were two different sized scoops, one custom-built and consisting of a hemispherical iron bowl on a short, wooden handle, the other a small, solid-brass saucepan worth many yuppie-style rounds of drinks by today's antique value standards. The first one served as my tin hat when playing at Tommies and Huns.

With a little difficulty I could raise any of the several bin-lids and rest them back agains the wall, then at full stretch on tiptoes could lean inside and revel in plunging my hands and arms into the contents. The varying smells and textures were each savoured in turn, ranging from the coarsely-ground pulses to the sensuous smoothness of the flour. There were particular games to be played too, such as making egg timers with my clenched fist or burying make-believe prizes in the bran then allowing myself lucky dips to see what I might retrieve. This last game proved to be a success until I tried it with a penny and a halfpenny in the flour, not realising the quicksand qualities involved. I dared not tell Father in case he fell to reflecting on whether or not the coins could negotiate the full length of some prized animal without predjudice to the beast's health.

It was a common sight to see the end-products of the bin-room being carried across the yard to the waiting occupants of stable, cowshed or pigstye; advance notice of breakfast time would have reached all concerned by breeze-borne wafts during mixing, and confirmation by the approach of footsteps and tell-tale bucket noises. Some loads were carried using a wooden yoke across the shoulders, the buckets suspended from the chains at either end see-sawing gently up and down like finely-balanced Scales of Justice.

Still more of the undercover food requirements for the livestock were kept in the adjoining small barn. Here were heaps of turnips and pig-potatoes, sacks of locust-bean pods and a wooden barrel of treacle, whilst at one end was an open hay-loft reached by climbing a well-worn ladder. The turnips were converted into finger-sized pieces by feeding them into the hopper of a hand-operated turnip cutter. Those chips of yellow flesh were delicious, as also were the sweet, crunchy pods of the locust beans. Together with licks of the thick, dark-brown treacle they formed gourmet snacks for me, stimulating the taste buds to appeal for further sampling.

After the barn came a large gate leading to our second paddock-cum-orchard and to the rear of another row of sheds, set at right-angles to the last ones. There was first an open cartshed and then a double pigsty, its occupants' main aims in life being to golup-down pig-swill, sleep, make smells, or emit rude grunts and indulge in bad behaviour in general. The nearest I might get to being lyrical about these animals would be when talking of their pink piglets. Often there would be a weakly runtlet in a litter which required bottle-feeding, and when this job fell to my lot I would take amusement in uncurling the tightly coiled tails of those cheeky little urchins then watch them flick back like the hairspring of a watch. Meanwhile in the stye their ample-figured mother would lie as contentedly on her side as Wodehouse's Empress of Blandings, her piggywigs jostling for position at the milk bar like tipplers at closing time.

The pig-swill was kept in a huge vat alongside the sties, being replenished by every conceivable waste product of kitchen, garden and orchard, supplemented by meal etc. from the bin-room and kept to a soup-like consistency by lashings of pond water. This revolting and sour-smelling brew would be ladled into buckets by Father, and one day during this operation he turned to find his waistcoat had disappeared from the sty wall, the resident porker having taken it for a tasty *hors d'oeuvre*.

I am reminded of a fanciful bar-story which I would relate years afterwards when in the RAF – especially after liberal helpings of my own particular swill. My tale was that after years of experiments in the selective feeding of pigs, Father eventually perfected a diet which resulted in streaky bacon reading "Home cured" through every slice!

There was another outhouse next door to the pigsties which also was devoted largely to the processing of pig food and known as the boiler room. This name came from the large iron cauldron and fire used for boiling what were called pig potatoes, these being any too small or otherwise unsuited for kitchen use. We children found them delicious when fished out straight after boiling, risking burnt fingers and mouths as we rubbed off the skin and gobbled down mouthfuls while still piping hot. I can think of no reason why those potatoes should taste different from any other boiled ones, but the general environment made them special – like picnic food.

From outside the boiler room a short, steep slope led down to the edge of the millpond where cattle and horses could drink, but I shall return to the mill and its surrounds after talking about the rest of the farm buildings. We have swung nearly full circle around the main yard, except for a large, nondescript wooden shed which served as a garage for Father's Triumph combination motorbike and sidecar, and also housed the trap used when making social visits. Past the door to the garden then Jack's kennel, and we are once again at the back (front!) door of the house.

Before leaving that yard I should mention an astonishing scene which I once witnessed there which was not intended for my innocent young eyes, but then it was not planned either. I chanced to be in the bin-room one day when suddenly I became aware of pandemonium out in the yard. There were urgent shoutings, bellowings, skidding of soft hooves on cobblestones, and thrashing sticks. An excited bull had leapt over the wall towards a cow which had strayed into the yard, and in two shakes of a nose-ring I was witnessing the rape of Lucrece (or whatever the unfortunate's name was). No amount of cudgel-thwacking by Father and Frank had the slightest effect on the lusty, taurine Don Juan, bent on having his wicked way like a sailor on shore leave after a long voyage. The reluctant Jezebel could do little other than stand with her tongue out thinking of England, while I slunk back into the bin-room sensing that some hitherto withheld mystery had inadvertently been part-revealed before it was intended. I had heard talk of bulls 'serving' cows, but had always pictured this as being some kind of table service such as an immaculately-clad butler would provide. In the event, what I had just seen was certainly no immaculate conception!

I mentioned earlier a stockyard which lay eastwards off the main yard. In fact we called it the crewyard, though just why I do not know; doubtless some readers may know the derivation of that term. Like the main yard, it was almost entirely enclosed by walls or buildings, including one side of the house. The farm buildings around it comprised stables, cowsheds and loose boxes for calves or sheep, and the animals housed there were the source of the manure which lay in a great heap in the centre of the yard. That heap seldom stopped steaming throughout the whole year, as countless billions of bacteria (many times the human population of the entire world) steadily converted it to a more wholesome state for fertilising the land.

A spring-fed drinking trough stood against one wall, and here cows and horses would suck in huge thirst-quenching

draughts, making unmannerly noises like the last gallon of water rushing out of a bath-tub. With thirsts slaked, the horses would generally turn and walk away; the cows were more likely to linger on, exhaling sickly sweet breath in great gusts from their wide nostrils, selfishly fending off would-be lesser-fry drinkers with half-hearted thrusts of their horns.

The bulky storage heaters of all those bovine bodies kept the cowsheds beautifully warm in winter, and this, coupled with the steady crunching of a dozen pairs of jaws could induce a relaxed state bordering on the soporific. However, it payed to remain alert when passing the cows' rear ends, as there was a danger of being deluged by more than one variety of effluent and with a minimum of warning. One rule was to avoid passing behind a cow with a hacking cough, as same-day dry-cleaning had not yet arrived.

Of course from a strictly economic point of view, the cows were simply very efficient machines for the rapid conversion of vegetable matter into milk, and as no more can be got out than is put in, it was important to keep them well fed. The racks at horn level were kept full of sweet-smelling hay, and the mangers below with tasty mangolds, turnips or cabbage, plus an occasional treat of lip-smacking cow-cake. A lump of rock salt lay at one end of the manger, to be licked as required for medicinal purposes. It was a sort of cosy-gentleman's/gentlewoman's agreement between farmer and cow – I will keep you well supplied with rich food if you will let me sit with my head resting against your thigh and take certain liberties with you!

Adjacent to the cowsheds was the main, general-purpose barn which lay under the granary I mentioned earlier on. All around inside were the minor trappings of agriculture. Odd lengths of rope and twine hung from the stout beams and posts, scythes, forks and rakes lay safely up against the walls, while wheelbarrows and sack-lifters awaited calls to duty. On window-sills and ledges lay old bottles and tins part-full of unspecified liquids and congealed animal medicaments, alongside broken bits of carborundum sharpening-stones, rusty sheep-shears and the like. A good way of passing an idle half-hour was to rummage through one of several old boxes of oddments lying around, as invariably some fresh gem would come to light. No attempt seemed to have been made to sort them out, so typically they contained a jumble of nuts, bolts, screws, washers, springs, bicycle clips, puncture outfits, buckles, straps and as many other assorted items as would fill many pages of an ironmonger's catalogue. A liberal admixture of cobwebs, chaff, rust and dust made a sift-through even more exciting, with finds like coloured marbles, military buttons, an old penknife or shepherd's crook turning up often enough to reward my searches.

Sometimes in the barn I would relax on a pile of sacking or stretched out on the old bench, watching some small disc of sunlight work its way slowly around, picking out familiar objects or elongating into long shafts as it alighted slantwise on its objective. At such quiet times I might hear sounds otherwise masked by my own activities – a mouse somewhere around or the owl ruffling his feathers high up in a dark alcove.

On wet days or at other times when work on the land was impracticable, the barn was used for various rainy-day jobs. Thatch-pegs for corn stacks would be made from hazel-tree branches, holes in potato sacks mended or the potatoes themselves riddled free of dirt, sorted and graded. This was a time for general discussion of farming matters – concern about delayed sowing of corn, the merits of nitrate of soda as a crop dressing, or rumours of swine fever somewhere across the country. The exhaustion of those topics would bring the relish of straightforward gossip – was the housemaid at Hardwick really serious about Fred Hardcastle or just leading him on, and had anyone ever noticed the minister's bicycle outside the back door of Rookswood Cottage?

The barn once played a part in rough justice meted out by Father to a casual labourer he found guilty of petty theft. On finding that the man was habitually stealing several eggs a day and secreting them on top of a beam in readiness for a last-minute reach-up and quick pocketing of the loot on his way out at night, Father laid his plan. After ensuring that the eggs had been hidden as usual, he daubed them liberally with ripe pig manure and red paint, then later hid nearby when the unsuspecting pilferer was due to leave work. With perfect timing Father emerged just as the man had reached up and taken the eggs, leaving him little option but to put the foul mess quickly into his pocket and mount his cycle, pedalling off embarrassed, red-faced and indeed caught red-handed!

The farmstead included yet a third yard, known as the stackyard and lying straight across the narrow road. Apart from its obvious use as a site for the stacks of hay and corn, it had a large open cartshed and ample parking space for such carts and farm implements as could not be housed under cover.

The whole stackyard had a semi-abandoned air, as much of it consisted of stony or impacted ground which encouraged the growth of weeds around the vehicles and machinery parked seemingly at random all over the place. Beds of tall nettles almost engulfed ploughs and rollers, rosebay willow-herb thrust skywards through the tines of the hayrake, and the chain harrow lay camouflaged by coarse grass. A sudden breeze would release an airborne drop of thistledown parachutes, and the crossing of an innocent looking stretch of ground could reveal a minefield of discarded ploughshares, heavy chains and cast-iron cogwheels.

The equipment kept in the shelter of the tall cartshed itself was luckier, and in general consisted of the various wooden carts and waggons, and other items more vulnerable to the weather, i.e. the corn and hay harvesting machines. This place was a favourite undercover playground for me in wet weather, well away from Mother's surveillance. As often as not I would play at being the driver, sitting in command on a tumbril holding imaginary reins or enjoying the springy bounce of the all-metal seat of the Massey Harris corn reaper. When tired of that I could poke around the sheaf-binding mechanism of the reaper, marvelling at its skills but never able to fathom out how it could have metal fingers and thumbs which actually tied knots.

A good game to play with Philip was hide-and-seek in the stackyard, or simply chasing one another in and around the network of alleyways formed by the several stacks, resulting in Keystone Cop situations. Rats and mice lived in the corn stacks, hence the cats frequently hung around there. Knowing this, when the cat Tittums died of old age I took her body along a track leading away from the stackyard and buried her in a quiet spot, making regular visits to lay flowers on her grave right until we moved from Newbound Mill Farm.

The old water mill from which the farm took its name lay at the south-east corner of the farmstead, behind the garden. Naturally its derelict state simply begged for children to play there, though we had been warned of the dangers. I feel sure that it must have lain unused for generations, so never having seen it work makes it more difficult to remember clearly the details of its layout, but certain things remain in my memory.

The mill lay on two levels, the upper storey being reached from the dam end whilst the lower one was built on ground sloping away towards the orchard. Inside was a complex of huge wooden shafts, gearwheels, hoppers, trapdoors, ropes, posts and beams – and of course the massive horizontal millstones themselves. At least one rope stretched up through both storeys, allowing the miller to tug it for controlling some operation or other from whichever level he chanced to be on. Another rope provided for powered hauling-up of sacks through a trapdoor in the floor. One clear memory I have is of burning my hands severely through sliding down one of the ropes from top to bottom of the mill – an object lesson in friction which I have never forgotten! The atmosphere inside the old mill always reminded me of the song which we sang regularly with great gusto as Teversal school:

In Hans' old mill his three black cats
Watch the bins for the thieving rats,
Whisker and claw, they crouch in the night,
Their five eyes smouldering green and bright:
. . . .
Jekkel, and Jessup, and one-eyed Jill.

Outside was the huge waterwheel, constantly traversed by a steady leak of water through the worn sluice-gates though never actually turned by it. During our games, the dog Jack and I would sometimes stand looking down into the mill-race; I was both fascinated and frightened by the thought of falling into the deep shaft and being drowned without the slightest hope of anyone hearing my cries for help from the bottom of that fern-lined well. By some accident of layout there was always a fine mist of water droplets hanging there in the air, and by another trick occasional shafts of sunlight produced miniature rainbows embedded in the spray, giving a hint of fairyland.

Water to turn the mill wheel ran underground from the dam only a few paces away. The dam formed the bulbous end of a long stretch of backwater made by diverting part of the main stream which carried on to run under the old bridge. With no further requirement as a source of power for grinding corn, that pond now served as a highway for ducks,

a watering-hole for cattle, a bath-tub for sheep, a playground for boys, and a breeding-ground for pondweed, rushes, minnows, frogs, dragonflies and a whole catalogue of other fauna and flora. The huge ramparts of earth originally piled up to contain that mass of water now formed a pleasant, grassy slope where we would lie basking in the sun when no better idea occurred to us.

The mill-pond nearly claimed a victim from our family when my baby sister Gladys somehow escaped everyone's attention one day. She toddled round the back of the garage shed, wearing my school cap over her eyes, and fell into the pond at the deep end. By sheer good fortune, Father found her just in time as she re-surfaced, and all turned out well.

The whole farm was small by present-day standards, being only a hundred acres or so of land stretching from the bridge and along either side of the Teversal road. It was known as a mixed farm – part grassland, part arable, with livestock to match. Thus the hay fed the horses that pulled the plough that turned the earth that grew the turnips which fed the cows who manured the fields where grew the grass which made the hay that fed the horses who lived on the farm that Joe ran!

The agricultural or pastoral scene is fine as viewed via a Constable painting, a Hardy novel, a Shelley poem or a Beethoven composition – and I subscribe to the beauties of all such media for titillating the mind's eye – but the realities are often less pleasant and more banal. "The ploughman homeward plods his weary way" just about sums up the sheer drudgery of walking on or working with actual clods of soil all day – not your cake-fresh, compost-textured stuff of a cosy garden border, but the sour-dough reality of soggy ploughland. Obviously I speak not as a ploughman (though I was on occasion called on to lead horses along the furrow) but as a one-time, penny-an-hour hireling on other work which entailed trudging over the land, handling it, getting thoroughly cold, dispirited and messed up by it, and carrying diver's-boot weights of it around for hours on end. To be a farmer's boy was not, to my way of thinking, a way of life to be recommended to a growing lad – a well-breeched farmer himself perhaps, but not his ragged-trousered lackey.

The particular cold, clammy and back-breaking jobs I had in mind when blowing off steam were the cleaning and topping-and-tailing of turnips, mangolds and sugar-beet. In the case of sugar-beet there were extra penalties to bear, for either chopping off too much white flesh or leaving on too much green both invited Father's displeasure, as in each case it meant money lost when it came to payment by the factory. Cut fingers through careless moments were commonplace, but at least Father would offer me the sympathy of jocular remarks such as "You're like a toad with gloves on!"

Hoeing and singling of root crops were other jobs which I disliked intensely, for not only was it back-aching work but also a gang system was adopted, involving three or four of us being told to keep abreast as we each worked our way down a row of turnips or mangolds. At my age I could scarcely be expected to keep up with the others, but apparently still was, so on dropping behind I would become the butt of taskmaster-like reprimands, sarcasm or (as a last resort) cajoling, but all to little effect, for if I wished to try and prove myself as good as or better than my elders, then it would be on battlegrounds and with weapons of my own choosing (chemical warfare?!).

A more endurable job was stone picking, the aim being to free grassland of objects likely to damage the blades of the grass-cutting machine. The company was congenial, the terrain reasonably pleasant, and there was a definite incentive as Father paid us by the bucketful. Our gatherings were tipped onto little cairns made by the hedgerows, and as each load was discharged Father made some secret note of our earnings. An old country tradition said that stones 'grew' out of the ground, and scientifically unsound as that idea may be, it certainly seemed strange that each year a fresh crop was ready to be gathered. As potential financial beneficiaries, did Philip and I know the answer? No comment!

The voracious appetites of certain birds at seedtime and harvest could be ruinous to a small farmer, and various ways of countering this problem have been tried for centuries. At Newbound Mill we stuck to three methods – scarecrows, clappers and the occasional firing of a twelve-bore shotgun over the feeding birds. Each seemd to be of very limited value, but at least the making of scarecrows was fun. Hilda would join with us in trying to make as lifelike yet comical scarecrows as possible, and each one of these dummies was credited with a personality of his own. The clappers we used were very simple devices, consisting of a short but stout wooden bat to which a matching flap was loosely hinged by a leather thong. The incredible racket produced by shaking the clappers was in the nature of a two-edged weapon, for although it undoubtedly scared hell out of the birds, any temporary dereliction of duty by the operator could quickly be detected a good mile away by the overseer, and retribution would follow on the return to base. I nearly forget a further method used – the deterrent of hanging up dead crows like felons at Tyburn, *pour encourager les autres*.

Haymaking sounds fun, the term itself carrying overtones of some kind of jolly romping, and also don't we talk of making hay while the sun shines? That latter phrase probably contains the root of what finally caused an aversion to farming for Philip and I – the last straw or wisp of hay, so to speak. Too often the sun did not shine after grass cutting, and the yellowing-green swathes lay damp and mouldering on the ground, so they had to be turned and tossed, then soon turned and tossed again unless the crop was to be ruined. This was where we came in and unfortunately when we didn't go out, for the hay could be turned by us only when the weather brightened up and of course when we were not at school – precisely the time when our fellows were out and about enjoying themselves. I am not suggesting that Father was unduly hard on us in the circumstances, as it was virtually a necessity for him to use us in that way if he was to survive as a farmer, but the full implications of his situation did not occur to us at that age. In the event, we fell secretly to calling him "old sun and wind" – a reference to the criteria which he used aloud for judging in which direction the hay was to be turned on each occasion.

There was generally far more fun to be had during the corn harvest, a time of relief and rejoicing at the conclusion of the hard work, misfortunes and uncertainties of the farming year. The old Harvest Festival hymns say it all, from "The sower went forth sowing, the seed in secret slept" to "Fair waved the golden corn in Canaan's pleasant land" and ending with "All is safely gathered in, ere the winter storms begin."

The operation could begin only after Father had assessed the critical factors of corn ripeness, immediate and longer-term weather prospects etc., and then given the go-ahead for an actual start. First a six-foot wide way had to be scythed all around the cornfield, to provide access for the horse-drawn 'binder' (the corn reaping and binding machine). This job was started around daybreak, the dew serving as a lubricant for the smooth, slicing action of the wickedly-keen blades, Frank and Father working together rythmically in a staggered echelon as corn with a sparse intermingling of scarlet poppies fell in neat swathes. Blue was the sky, golden the corn, sweet the cool morning air, and bounteous the quiet smile of Nature reflected in the grain-filled ears of wheat and hedgerow fruits and berries.

Soon the binder would be clattering around the field, drawn by the willing Darkie and Prince, Father perched aloft with his overview of horses, oscillating knife, flailing rotary arms and line of ejected sheaves. When on its best behaviour, the machine would cut a width of corn then sweep it back onto a moving canvas bed, compress it into a bundle tied with twine then throw it clear onto the ground. The fly in the ointment was Father's enforced purchases of second-hand equipment, resulting in frequent stoppages when the machine threw tantrums instead of sheaves. Someone (myself at times) then had to bind the trail of untied bundles with ropes of twisted straw, while Father solved his knotty problem!

The sheaves were next propped up against each other in tens or twelves to form stooks, so as to keep them dry and in readiness for loading and carting away. The men could easily grab one sheaf in each hand, knock their heads together and leave them standing, whereas I had to drag along one at a time. It was pleasant enough work, but very hard on young bare arms already rendered sensitive through exposure to the fierce sunlight, so by nightfall the skin could be very scratched and sore.

Our run-on-a-shoestring farm had neither the equipment nor labour to do everything just as per the book, hence corn was brought home for stacking in whichever type of cart was available, with or without someone to lead the horses during loading up in the field. Use of a two-wheeled tumbril meant that care had to be taken to keep the weight reasonably over the axle, for an extreme out-of-balance situation when going uphill could result in the poor horse literally being lifted off its feet. As to shortage of labour, with no one to lead the horse a succession of 'Gees' and 'Whoas' was relied on to move it on and then stop just where required as each group of corn stooks was loaded; this inevitably lead to misunderstandings between man and horse, resulting in frayed tempers on both sides. This is where I came in when not at school, but even leading a horse calls for minor bits of

know-how if things are to go smoothly: hold his bridle close to his mouth so that he cannot nibble you, allow for the inertia of the load when stopping, and keep from under those feet! This latter observation stems from an unforgettable experience involving Prince, for he once stopped with one outsized, iron-clad hoof on my sparrow-like toes, looking stubbornly ahead as I yelled and thumped his flank. The crushing pain felt as though my toes were gripped in some Iron Maiden form of torture clamp. When finally Prince was persuaded to move, I remember staring in disbelief at the imprint of my foot in the solid earth, like an exaggeration from a Popeye cartoon!

Stacking of the corn sheaves was an art akin to building a house, and I gained a little insight into it when helping on top of the stacks. A good foundation layer was important, though even afterwards each sheaf had to be positioned to the best advantage if the end result of a stable, well-shaped stack was to be achieved. There was little opportunity for those on the stack to pause and consider, for the pitchers below plied them continuously with more sheaves, everyone anxious to ensure that all was safely gathered in, in case the weather broke or fate intervened in some other unforeseen way. Sometimes a succession of twisting sheaves would appear over the stack skyline like salmon leaping up a weir. The top layers were tapered-in to form a sloping roof, and as the final thatch-peg was driven into the last-stack, it really was Harvest Home for yet another year.

If, in the calendar of farming events there had been an award for Entertainment of the Year, then the clear winner would have been Threshing Day. The promoters got plenty of advance publicity from the slow procession through the countryside of the threshing tackle – a long, box-like structure on solid iron wheels, towed by a sort of Puffing Billy steam-engine. Walking alongside or riding would be the threshing gang, as ragged and characterful-looking lot as you might expect to find on a Mayor of Casterbridge film set.

There was a bustling activity in our stackyard as the equipment was pushed, pulled, levered and chocked in position during much shouting of orders, while that pot-bellied monster stood arrogantly whistling through its teeth, knowing that shortly it would play the leading role in the show. When things got under way, the air was filled with dust, noise and smoke from the engine. Water was sucked up through a fat pipe with its nozzle lying in our tin bath near the engine and then converted into steam which turned the flywheel to whirl the belt-drives which spun the pulleys, so bringing to life the cranks, levers, drums, arms and beaters inside that huge box, each with its appointed task.

The sheaves were tossed from the stack to a man on top of the contraption who cut the bands while his partner fed a large, gobbling mouth in the roof of the machine. The internal choppings, beatings, winnowings and siftings resulted in delivery of the various end-products from ducts, flaps and chutes into sacks and piles around and under the machines. Men came and went in all directions, carrying heavy sacks of grain, sheet-loads of chaff and bucketfuls of alien weed seeds, while a giraffe-like elevator carried the decapitated straw up to the men making a new stack. As usual I had my own job, replenishing the tin bath with water carried from the horse-trough across the road. As I neared the engine the noise was deafening, the workers often straining to hear one another with hands cupped to ears, the fine dust and coal smoke clinging to sweaty faces, bringing sore and bloodshot eyes to all and sundry.

There would be a welcome break from the hard work, dust and clamour at 'snap time', when from grimy haversacks and knotted red handkerchiefs would come hunks of bread and cheese, to be eaten seated up against the stacks and washed down with swigs of cold tea from screw-top bottles, adam's-apples rising and falling with each delicious gulp, finishing with the obligatory belch and wiping of mouth with the back of the hand.

With luck the operation would be over before nightfall, the hired labourers shuffling into the kitchen to be payed and receive the traditional quart of beer and plateful of food. Amongst them was a man who bore witness to one of the several dangers associated with that work, one sleeve of his tattered jacket being tucked into the pocket, redundant for all time.

At this time of the year, little remained to be done in the stackyard from now on except the sawing of logs, using either the large, two-handled cross-cut saw or the smaller bow-saw. This last-named tool was looked on by me with a degree of reverence not accorded to others, for it was said to be of Canadian origin, evoking pictures of Father out there in his ear-flapped beaver cap, scorning the threats from frostbite, drunken lumberjacks and grizzly bears alike.

The leaves would fall, rain, fog and snow come as relative quiet enveloped barn, mill and fields, the animals snug in their frowsty sheds and stables. But when winter comes, can spring be far behind? Another farm year was about to dawn.

9

A CHAT WITH THE ANIMALS

For as long as I can remember, my relationship with animals has been governed by the view that they have as much right to be around as we have. Having said that, I always have guilty feelings about killing vermin and the hypocrisy of on the one hand seeing lambs as the gambolling heralds of spring and at other times as ideal companions for mint sauce. However, my basic love of animals still remains, though I have never yet got round to asking for the vegetarian dish of the day at any restaurant or pub.

Talking of pubs, how nice it would be to have the gift of

being able to talk with the animals and to meet up with some of those furred and feathered friends of long ago – and what more appropriate place than the Nag's Head at Pleasley! So here we go through the looking glass for a pint or two of nostalgia in a Disney World fantasy land.

There they all sit around over their drinks or lounge with one elbow on the bar, though one of them slinks out as I enter, knowing that otherwise I might have cut him dead. Let's face it, pigs are indeed pigs, with dirty faces, shoes, smells and habits; they have no table manners, a limited vocabulary and slovenly diction – so goodbye Percy Porker!

With a zoological mixing of metaphors I might say that cows are a different kettle of fish, and I am glad to spot my old friend Daisy, who has at last taking to wearing a bra. I slip into a spare seat beside her as she sips her milk stout, though it is a full minute before I can gain her attention as she stares vacantly ahead while chewing her salted peanuts, apparently ruminating on life in general and nothing in particular. Did she remember how, as leader of the herd, she would claim her prerogatives of the first drink at the trough and a snatched mouthful of tit-bits as she passed each manger on entering the cowshed? Yes, she agreed with a lazy flick of one ear, and wasn't it a laugh when my father caught me riding her when bringing the cows home from the field one afternoon at milking time. He said it would spoil her milk yield, but she hadn't really minded as it gave a feeling of companionship. She reminded me about the incident with her friend Lucy and Billy Bull, saying it served her right for always making calf's eyes at him across the safety of Three Acre Meadow, only to stand him up on that date behind the cowshed. A man can only stand so much teasing, then something's got to give!

I asked Daisy why she and her friends all used to face the same way in the field when grazing or lying down chewing the cud. Ah well, she said, that was all a question of wind up their petticoats, if I saw what she meant. I did. Now could she ask me a question – why did we milkers sometimes make sudden grabs at her offside leg? I hastened to explain that this was not undue familiarity, but merely a kind of wrestler's lock to prevent her nearside leg from kicking the bucket as we felt her muscles flex to stamp in order to dislodge some annoying fly.

At this point I turned to see Gilbert, Prince and Darkie approaching our table, and after much back slapping and "How are you old horse!" preliminaries they sat down beside us with their pints of bitter, obviously in bibulous high spirits. They began by ribbing Daisy as to whose manure was considered the best for putting on rhubarb, and Gilbert (always the wag) sent Daisy into a fit of the giggles by saying he preferred custard on his! Prince countered by remarking that you can't beat the old 'uns, and then we got down to more-serious reminiscing.

What about the time when Darkie slipped on the wet cobbles in his stable, falling in such an awkward position in that confined area that it took several hours of discussions, ineffective exhortations and flounderings before eventually he was assisted to his feet by means of a broad belly-band fastened to ropes and pulleys suspended from the roof beams.

Gilbert was next subjected to comradely macho humour by Prince and Darkie regarding his pansyfied trotting between the shafts of the trap: he merely revealed his toothy dentures with a suave grin, observing that only thick clod-hoppers like them could fail to recognise his postured effeminacy as a way of escaping dragging ploughs along or pulling muck-carts around. Anyhow, if he was like they said, how come he was the one who caused the Mother memsahib to turn blushingly away with a remark to the boys about the hot weather, on that day he fell to daydreaming about the winsome little filly he had met over their nosebags of oats at

Chesterfield market?

Prince hurriedly changed the subject by recounting the time he had led my father a lively dance one spring morning after the halter had been slipped on to lead him in from the paddock, Father mounting him to save walking to the farmyard. I said I remembered the incident well, for I was just walking past the paddock on my way to school when Father appeared suddenly to have taken leave of his senses, galloping bareback twice around the small field with yells and caperings like a cowboy at a hick-town rodeo. I spent much of that day at school pondering on my parent's sudden strange behaviour, but on returning home I learned that Father had not been showing off but simply clinging on for dear life. As Prince said, if you feed a horse too much corn you must accept the risk of him demonstrating a trick or two learned as a colt.

Next Darkie chipped in with a reminder of how at times he had been forced to take his medicine; first the cord of a 'twitch' was twisted around his upper lip to bring him under control and force him to open his mouth, following which he would be 'drenched' with liquid medicine via a spout made from a cow's horn, or a golf-ball sized pill was blown down his throat using a long tube. What a life! And what about shoeing said Gilbert, all those trial fittings by burning-in the red-hot shoes, then having them fastened on by nails driven through your own toe-nails.

Here the conversation was interrupted by the cats Fluff and Tittums mincing over with their cream sherries to join us. Did I, asked Fluff, recall the way Frank and I would tease them when they wandered into the cowshed at milking time? One of us would hold each of them up in turn, to squint through the latch-hole of the cowshed door while the other hosepiped a jet of milk straight from the teat into her eye. The laugh was partly on us, she said, as they loved licking the warm, creamy milk off their dripping wet faces. This

reminded me to tell them of Mother's little ploy to induce them not to run away from Newbound Mill Farm when we first moved there. The cats had travelled from our previous farm in separate baskets, and on arrival each had her front paws smeared liberally with best butter, so that while licking it off they had time to reflect on the possibility that this strange new environment might not be such a bad place to live in after all. This was certainly tastier fare than the meal table leftovers which had formed their regular diet at their last home.

I went on to mention Tittums' strange habit of sleeping on the very edge of the kitchen table. The fact that on several occasions she startled herself by falling off while asleep never seemed to cure her of this dangerous practice. Well, she retorted, what about you trying to accelerate this event by holding close to my bare backside a delayed-action 'cartridge' made from smouldering brown paper and a toy-pistol cap. The tricks some boys got up to! Seeing my glum look of contrition at this censorious reminder, she extended what appeared to be the paw of friendship, though after a couple of seconds my knee felt the mailed fist of her claws inside the velvet glove.

Fluff declared that she missed the whole darned lot of us more than she could say, and they could keep all their Kitto Kat and Lushus Likko tinned rubbish for one cracked plateful of good old rabbit stew. Having let off a suitable head of steam, both pussies sidled off towards a newly arrived pair of ginger toms who leant on the bar toying with their G & Ts while casting appraising eyes over the local talent.

Suddenly I became aware of an affectionate, melting look from a pair of female eyes across the crowded room – the kind of stuff that dreams are made of. Recognising those twin, limpid pools as belonging to the collie bitch Gyp, I walked over to get reacquainted. After a quick nuzzle, we got to talking of those days of sheep, rabbits and rats, and evenings by the fireside. Her most vivid memory was of the time she was nearly drowned through poking her head inside an empty milk bucket for a sly lick-around. By chance the handle had stayed erect, but Gyp's intrusion snapped it down like a mousetrap, at which she panicked and tried to run off. I myself was a witness to the scene as she dashed round the yard with increasing terror of this self-generated pandemonium; just as she rounded a corner apparently intent on escaping this harrying monster by jumping into the mill-pond, she was intercepted by Frank, this probably saving her life.

"Talking of rats," said the black mongrel Jack sitting nearby, "I've still got the scar". Completely puzzled, I stared at him awaiting some clue, but as soon as he pointed to his damp nose it all came back to me. The scene was a traditional one, threshing day as the last few layers of sheaves were being tossed up onto the machine, workers and onlookers alike all armed with sticks, stones and cudgels, alert for the fleeing rats. During the general confusion of shouts, thwacks and darting rodents I saw my chance and brought my stick smartly down – on Jack's nose! The blood gushed out of a gaping wound as poor Jack spun round and round in agony, his pitiful yelps bringing an instant end to the day's enjoyment – a bloodied nose indeed!

Jack growled quietly at the memory, and an old, blue-rinsed ewe instinctively edged away nervously, setting her hooped earrings swinging like tiny pendulums. I glanced up at her and said "Excuse me, but don't I know you?" "You ought to ducky," she said, pausing for a sip of her Babycham as she eyed me over the rim of the glass, "at least your Dad did. Took the very coat off my back he did, though not without a struggle I can tell you!" Now I remembered, for she it was who literally had given Father a run for his money at sheep shearing time. I was turning the handle on the cast-iron pedestal of the shearing machine while Father used the clippers at the end of a universally-jointed arm. I believe the poor animal in the barber's chair was suffering just as I generally did under Father's hand on such occasions, but after a couple of nicks which drew blood she decided that enough was enough. With a deft twist or two she was free of Father's wrestling hold and away across the field. With the cape-like fleece flying from her neck and Father in hot pursuit, the scene was like Mephistopholes fleeing from Gabriel, with good finally triumphing over evil.

Having wrung the last drops of amusement from that episode, the ewe said that surely I must also remember her younger companion standing sheepishly by her side, as we had spent several cosy evenings together by the fire. This young female turned out to be an orphan lamb raised on the bottle, who at night would be bedded down in a clothes basket on the hearth, an alarm clock wrapped in an old blanket taking the place of her mother's comforting heartbeats. She became so attached to humans that even when fully grown up she would always leave the rest of the flock to join whichever of us happened to be around.

Fortunately even the old ewe spared my blushes by refraining from any mention of two barbarous-sounding operations performed on each springtime batch of new lambs, so for the record I will refer briefly to them myself. Firstly the lambs' tails would be docked with a single stroke of Father's ultra-sharp jack-knife, and I can vouch for the surprising fact that immediately after the wound was treated the lambs would resume their grazing as if nothing had happened. Happily they were unaware that by nightfall those severed appendages would have been the subject of appreciative comments from people enjoying that once-a-year delicacy – lambstail pie. Secondly there was castration of the male lambs, when Father would call on the services of a local shepherd; this wrinkle-faced expert made the incision with his penknife and the extraction with his teeth, spitting the would-be rams' incipient masculinity casually onto the grass. The ewe did get in one final dig at humans by reminding me of what a fine figure of a man her boyfriend the tup had proved himself to be when he butted my father up the backside. It happened one feeding time as Father was bent over shaking some kind of sheep food from a sack into their trough. Having let down his guard for a mere few seconds, suddenly he was knocked sprawling across the trough and spent the next few days limping around with a badly bruised thigh. The tup continued with his casual love affairs, his conquests advertising their liaisons by patches of yellow ochre on their backs.

I turned away from that old goat in sheep's clothing to join a cackling group of Buff Orpingtons and White Wyandottes, each pair of matchstick legs protruding from a froth of underskirts like those of the Miss Blenkinsop Formation Dancers. I had known most of them by name – Cissie, Gertrude, Millicent and so on – and could even recognise individual eggs by their shape, texture and colour, plain or speckled. None of these girls could tell the accepted female white lies regarding their age, as a coloured ring above one slim ankle denoted each one's year of birth. Not that the incestuous cockerel cared about such niceties as age or relationship, but as Grandma Wobblewottle noted with relief, he was not present tonight as this was strictly a hen party. She took me aside to say that now I had grown up she could reveal that Chanticleer had not been in perpetual training for the next Olympic 100-metre sprint, considering himself rather as a piece of hens' earth-moving equipment. In return I told that toothless hag how I had picked up much of their fowl language, learning to distinguish between such sounds and cadences as motherly chiding, chicken chat, plaintive self-talk, alarm, and much-repeated proclamations after egg laying.

Towards closing time the atmosphere at the Nag's Head had become boozily mellow, with raucous pleasantries being exchanged between man, bird and beast. The mongrel Jack's body language suddenly spoke of his intention to buttonhole me, as he weaved an unsteady few paces towards me past the singing Prince and Darkie, then stood rocking on his paws as a mouthful of Kimberley Ale half-missed its target and slopped down the front of my already stained cavalry twills. "D'gerknow," he slobbered, apparently looking at both of my ears at the same time, "one of my fleas sez his great-great grandad reckons what an irritated lad you was!" We leant laughingly against each other as more beer spilled over our shoes and splashed Fluff's fishnet tights, but even as she turned to give us the cold look treatment a Khaki Campbell drake climbed onto a chair and shouted "Order please!" What a wonderful evening it had been, he quacked, as everyone continued to pursue their own noisy private chats, and how nice to meet the young master again . . . waffle, cackle, waffle. "Speak for yourself, creep!" squealed Percy Porker who had crept back in unnoticed to the jug-and-bottle counter for a last quick one before they closed.

I felt a maudlin state coming on, and edged my way towards a side exit as the tears welled up. As I staggered through the door a five-second shimmering transformation turned the cool night of yesteryear into the hot mid-day of July the 4th, 1989. I was back through the looking glass into reality.

10

THE FRAGRANT COUNTRYSIDE

It may be said that Newbound Mill Farm lies in countryside which is not only outstandingly beautiful but also unusually historic. Only two miles to the west stands that magnificent Elizabethan seat of nobility aptly described by the couplet "Hardwick Hall, more glass than wall". Travel five miles east and you are in the Dukeries, on the edge of what remains of Sherwood Forest. If Robin Hood and his band of merry men did indeed exist – and there surely must at least have been outlaws like them in that vast expanse of woodland – then they are bound to have known this area. Perhaps Friar Tuck once baked venison pasties in some makeshift, rustic oven nearby, and Maid Marian may have cooled her dainty feet in our stream, sitting on the bank in the shade of the willows some six hundred years ago.

Every place-name within two or three miles' radius of the farm speaks of the rural England of Saxon and Viking days – Teversal, Hardwick, Rowthorn, Pleasley, Ashfield, Kirkby and Skegby. To the humble folk of those far-off times, living amid fields, trees and streams was a familiar, everyday experience, as it was for us in the 1920s; in contrast to that situation, for an increasing number of people today, the term countryside refers to an area outside of their normal orbit, to be visited purely as a leisure activity.

Pursuing that last thought a little further, on looking back I feel privileged to have lived in such times and circumstances as made day-to-day life a holiday by most people's standards. (By that reckoning, I suppose that our 'pleasures' and 'outings' lay in visiting urban jungles!). We did not consciously seek relaxation or the beauties of nature by rambling the fields and lanes – it just happened as we went about our daily routines.

The geography of our little territory was in itself pleasant enough, with no overwhelming majesty or level monotony, but simply a rolling gentleness with enough steepish rises to give it plenty of character. In fact the farm was situated near the start of far more exaggerated hills to the north-west, the old bridge lying directly on the Notts/Derbyshire border. Naturally the stream ran in a valley of sorts, so that the lane on one side led up a fairly steep hill to Pleasley village and in the opposite direction made a short, turning climb around our farmyard towards Teversal. That latter small hill was the source of great fun for Philip and myself, as it formed a racetrack down and around which we would hurtle in competition on our wooden, pram-wheeled, make-believe Bentleys and Alfa-Romeos. A long stretch of grassland just to the south of our home fields also rose up steeply to a ridge, forming a pleasing green vista dotted with the blacks, whites and browns of grazing cattle. That undulating area was traversed by twisting, narrow lanes which sometimes tunnelled their way through the foliage of overhanging trees and bushes, and by a criss-cross pattern of ancient footpaths whose origins lay in manorial rights-of-way traditions stretching back a thousand years or more. Those paths needed no signs such as are erected today, as they were well enough known and used as to preclude any serious arguments regarding trespassing, and we were countrywise enough to respect the crops and livestock of other farmers.

Consideration of all the trees, plants, flowers and fruits which graced every stretch of lane or footpath, clothed each field or hid shyly in corners or hedgerows sets me marvelling at the sheer volume of floral knowledge and country love we children accumulated in such a short time. I believe this to be a good example of learning without tears, for had this been designated 'Botany' and taught at school using Latin names and dry-as-dust terminology then I am certain that we children would never have picked up even a fraction of what we did. As it was, how could we fail to take note of that diverse range of shapes, colours, textures and perfumes which bore fascinating and easily-related names like lady's smock, shepherd's purse, coltsfoot, stinkhorn or bacon and eggs. Take the horse chestnut for example: everything about it is easy to remember and invites further exploration – its name (did horses eat the nuts?), the super-sticky buds on its winter skeleton, its luxurious, green spring clothing of leaves, the pinkish-white glory of its 'candles' which marked the latter half of each May, the cathedral-cool shade from summer heat, and the prickly cases which enclosed the ultra-smooth brown 'conkers' so eagerly sought after by boys in the autumn – a tree for all seasons. No wonder it inspired that universally remembered word-picture that so succinctly distills the quintessence of Old England: "Under the spreading chestnut tree the village smithy stands".

There are numerous examples of how most of those quaint or charming old names are so apt as to make it virtually impossible not to remember their subjects: thus weeping willows seemed to be doing just that, old man's beard could well be imagined on Father Time's chin, oak apples are remembered as being impostors which merely housed creepy-crawlies, whilst lords and ladies (bulls and cows to most of us) displayed projections so obviously, phallic and erect in their female counterparts that dirty-minded little boys would study and discuss these teaching aids with prurient interest.

This association of ideas applied in some way or another to virtually all of the commoner plants and flowers: some were notably connected with the seasons, had animal names, unique perfumes, could be played with, were sources of food or drink, objects of superstition, love tokens and so on. There were dog roses, catmint, cow parsley, oxlips, horsetails, coltsfoot, sheep's sorrel, goat willow, harebells, toadflax, birdsfoot trefoil, fat hen, hawkweed and cranesbill.

One challenge in early spring was to search the hedgerow banks to make a posy of exquisitely perfumed violets as a gift for your sweetheart. Later on she might grant you the favour of accompanying her on a 'bluebelling' excursion in the woods (a euphemism for allegedly naughty goings-on). At other times you might sit close together amid buttercups rejected by the cows, holding the tiny cups close under the other's chin and peering intently to determine whether or not there was a yellow reflection – supposedly an indication of a liking for butter. Picking of that other brilliant flower, the dandelion, was said to incur a risk of wetting the bed, though the mind boggles as to how on earth some old herbalist or other dreamed that one up!

Easter brought the fun of colouring the traditional hard-boiled eggs with a dye made from an infusion of gorse petals, and gathering the two types of willow catkins – the fluffy, round pussy-willows and the dangling lambstail ones, both varieties prized as floral decorations. As Christmas approached there was the thrill of searching for holly branches which actually bore the red berries, as there was a loss of face for any home without this seasonal adornment. Sprigs of mistletoe were usually provided by Father, who showed a marked reluctance to let us into the secret of on which particular apple tree they were to be found.

There were plenty of games to be played and much fun to be had with the various flowers, fruits and grasses, ranging from the painstaked fashioning of dainty flower-chains to the technique of blowing crude 'raspberries' from blades of grass stretched between the thumbs. Whistles were made from cow parsley stems and satisfyingly-loud bangs produced by bringing seed bladders smartly down onto the saliva-moistened back of the hand.

Materials were readily available for making a small armoury of weapons. At the pussyfooting end of the scale were the plaintain guns, made by looping the stems behind the seed head and pressing with the thumbnail till the harmless projectile flew into your victim's face. One step up in lethality were the stay-spring operated pistols mentioned in an earlier chapter, followed by the stingingly-accurate hawthorn berry blowpipes. At the top of the range was the primitive bow and arrow, constructed from a varying selection of branches and feathers.

Acorn cups attached to their stems served as elf-sized pipes, and certain grasses topped by interlocking segments were used for the game 'Grandmother, grandmother, jump out of bed!" Uninitiated young victims were invited to watch closely as granny leapt from her spiky four-poster, only to receive an eye-smarting flick under the nose!

An unsolved mystery concerned how cuckoo spit appeared, and anyhow what a filthy trick it was for a

seemingly pleasant bird to play – expectorating on a lady's smock! Whenever I heard the merry note of that evasive trickster I would be alert to try and catch it in the act, but without success. There were rumours that these frothy bubbles were not bird's spit at all, but I rejected those suggestions out of hand: they were not romantic enough!

I consider it only natural that I have tended to concentrate on the countryside as seen through boyish eyes, but Philip and I could share some outdoor activities with our elder sister Hilda. For example, the local annual flower shows included entries for wild flowers, in respect both of the best display and also for sheer numbers of different species gathered. Here we were well situated to comb the area for new specimens, though I do not recall our crammed-to-capacity two-pound jam jar collections receiving any standing ovations in those stifling marquees. At least Hilda was praised by friends and family for her pressed flowers, with some semblance of their living beauty preserved for many years to come between pages of the New Testament and the Book of Psalms.

Some of even the commonest plants were openly hostile, apparently to humans in particular, as animals seemed largely oblivious to their threats. Stinging nettles were determined to avoid conversion into tea or being used as vegetables, brambles formed in-depth barbed wire defences against raids on their berries, there was certainly not even a dog-rose without a thorn, and Scottish-looking thistles appeared intent on giving we young Sassenachs a hard time.

In spite of all our cultivated food from the farm, garden and orchards, there were still minor harvests of wild products to be gathered. Spring was a time for local excursions to pluck elder flowers and cowslips for making wine. Mother would rope in Hilda, Philip and myself to help, for pleasant enough as this task was, it needed an awful lot of flowers to produce even one bottle of wine. We would pause frequently to take Lilliputian sips of nectar from the tiny cowslip flowers, though from the back-tilt of head and loud sucking it could as well have been draughts of mead.

Father would sometimes arrive home from the fields carrying a slightly bulging, knotted red handkerchief, which usually meant mushrooms – real mushrooms, ranging up in size from drawer knobs to dinner plates. He would dump his small bundle dramatically on the table with a triumphant "There then!", waiting for the signs of approval bound to follow as our minds savoured the coming treat.

Late summer and early autumn brought the ripening of hedgerow fruits and berries – super-sour crabapples for jelly, ultra-tart sloes for wine, and purple-staining blackberries for those scrumptious pies and jams. There was something about blackberrying which set it above the rest for all-round enjoyment, in spite of the inevitable scratched arms, legs and faces. Mother would carry a large basket which formed the bulk container, this being topped up regularly from the enamelled tea-cans and string-handled jam jars which we children used for gathering the juice-laden berries. Father's walking-stick was used for thrashing down the nettles or hooking inaccessible branches nearer, often resulting in vicious backlashes which ripped and lacerated the flesh of anyone within range. Rival groups of gatherers would be encountered, with pretty girls at full stretch to reach the last, tantalising berry, providing equally tantalising glimpses of where no decent, serious-minded lad should be looking anyway!

At the expense of appearing trite or bumptiously patronising, I must say that Keats had got it right about autumn – all that mellow fruitfulness, conspiring with the sun to load and bless, overbrimmed honey cells and so forth – what a thoroughly observant chap he was!

Although there was plenty of other wildlife around for me to observe and enjoy, there were few of the larger animals to be seen in our area, though once a fox was guilty of breaking and entering a hen roost, murdering two poor Pertelots and causing grevious bodily harm to another. Of course there were sightings of lithe stoats and weasels darting across the lane or weaving sinuously in and out of the hedgerows, and occasional glimpses of shy field-mice, shrews and voles. Snorts and rustling sometimes told of where hedgehogs were foraging, and in certain fields sleek-coated moles played havoc with Father's grassland, goading him to bursts of trap-setting.

Few birds went unrecognised by we country lads in respect of their plumage, song, flight patterns, eggs and nesting habits, and some had local names such as 'spudgie' (sparrow) and 'spink' (chaffinch). Birds-nesting was a common hobby, though we observed a strict code of not disturbing sitting birds and taking only one egg from a nest, and never the last or only one.

There was of course that other juvenile sport of fishing the streams with net and jam jar, the usual catches being minnows, sticklebacks and miller's thumbs. The last-named were also known as bullheads, but I found them particularly repellant under either label: they seemd to be just a brutal-looking braincase, grossly underpowered. I must put on record the strange story of the fish that could read. While fishing near the bridge I picked up an empty salmon tin from the shallows – but not really empty, for curled up inside was a small but very much alive salmon-trout!

Caterpillars had a fascination for me, especially the ones that looked like gaudy Chinese dragons, undulating and twisting their way along as though the centrepiece of some festive procession. Show-offs of another sort were the water-boatman bugs which skated across the mill-pond; their ability to walk on water must surely be the envy of some current political leaders of at least one political persuasion.

Back to the subject of revolting-cum-fascinating

creatures, to mention that I place in this category the newts which lived in one field-pond, as I do most other antideluvian-looking, reptilian or slimy forms of life. Yet again, I could not totally resist their strange magnetism, and even mounted a grass-snake hunting expedition one spring – another of life's heroic failures. Before leaving the theme entirely, I must retail the story told in our family about a certain drunken yokel. He is said to have lain paralytic outside his cottage door for so long one night that when his long-suffering wife eventually discovered him at dawn, a snail-trail led right across the path and over his waistcoat-clad belly to the other side.

It is time to leave the Teversal countryside. Listening to Vivaldi's *Four Seasons* sometimes brings back patchy memories of it all: Mother lost in a silent, winter fog, with a succession of searchers swallowed up also; the sleeping black hedgerows suddenly awake and clothed in their spring greenery; drowsy summer afternoons violated by angry bluebottles; and my piquant, autumn memory of the blackberrying nymphets – so long ago!

11

IN ORCHARD AND GARDEN

Newbound Mill's grander days long ago were reflected in its two ancient orchards, one stretching down towards the old bridge and the other on the Teversal side of the farmstead. Perhaps they might be better described as fruit trees dotted around paddocks, for the animals habitually grazed there and the one on the bridge side served also as a rough-and-ready pleasure ground for various sports and other leisure activities. Some wealthier former occupants had left behind several discarded items of sports gear in a dusty attic, and over the next few years we made good use of all of them in our orchard playground.

Looking back, I would date those items as early or mid-Victorian, and one in particular had a distinctly Trollopian air about it, for it was a croquet set. It was still in its long wooden box, with a faded set of rules pasted inside the lid. Although now reduced to serving us for knock-around foolery in the rough orchard grass, who knows what visiting frock-coated cleric may once have handled those mallets; perhaps while sizing-up a shot he was also weighing-up his chances with some sweet, crinolined partner.

The same kind of musings could apply to two other of those items discovered – an old-fashioned tennis set and a hammock. Hilda sometimes used the latter, slung between two conveniently spaced younger trees, while we boys tried our best with those hopeless racquets and cumbersome net. Again, our predecessors in such usage must have been better placed than we: perhaps an elegant young girl dozing off on a warm summer afternoon, a calf-bound volume of Tennyson slipping from her hand as two heavily-moustached young bloods engaged in a pit-pat battle across the net, with the lady subconsciously in mind as the prize.

Those former occupants had left no cricket gear, so we used thatch-pegs for stumps and fashioned our own bats out of some chunk or other of wood, most of the work being done by Frank. The bats had no springs or other such luxuries, thus matching the other equipment and the venue in general. In any case we only used an old tennis ball, which often ended up floating down the stream forming one of the boundaries. When tired of arguing about whose turn it was to bat, we could pull stumps and play on the swings. There were two of these, hanging from apple-tree boughs which had obligingly branched off at near-horizontal angles, giving a less-than-perfect swinging motion which would not have suited a purist any more than the thatch-peg stumps. Who cared anyway?

You may soon ask what has all this really got to do with orchards? The answer is everything, for if these places cannot be enjoyed in ways other than sinking our teeth into the end-products, then we might just as well rely on the greengrocer. After all, whoever wrote "You'll be mine in apple-blossom time" hadn't got fruit in mind.

"By their fruits ye shall know them" the Bible tells us; yes,

and in the case of trees rather than people, by their blossom also, each tree a shade different from its fellows, ranging from snowy whites through tints of pink verging on red. At their best, and in the crystal-sharp air of the right May morning, the beauty of a single sprig of buds could almost hurt.

A little later, in June, a day would come when Mother decided it was time for an *al fresco* meal. An old table would be carried down the garden steps, set under a tree and then covered with a spotless linen cloth. Nearby a horse-blanket would be spread out on the grass and small cloths laid on it also. The viands were brought out in wicker baskets, and it was time to set to and enjoy ourselves, with spiders abseiling down from the tree to take a look. I preferred to sprawl on the grass, and found such trivialities as twig fragments on the sandwiches or a leaf landing in my teacup were small penalties to pay for the sheer fun of it all.

The courtship between bees and blossom was soon followed by the nuptials, signalled by the gentle showering of confetti petals which I would observe when looking from my bedroom window across towards the bridge. It was always a shotgun wedding for soon afterwards came what was traditionally regarded as christening of the fruit, on St Swithin's Day. I would inspect the young apples after that day, curious as to whether or not they looked any more grown-up – sadly, they never did.

It is easy for me to invent a mnemonic aid for memorising the stock varieties of fruits on our trees: "Victoria's Conference with the Russet-cheeked Granny Smith led Bramley and Newton to Wonder, sucking on their Blenheim Oranges." (Why did the damsons have such an awkward name as Merryweather, and the greengages choose to remain anonymous?). Corny? – well I did my best! I nearly forgot the cherries, but their name apart, that would be quite impossible for three main reasons: firstly their colours as they ripened from yellow through shades of red to a rich vermilion; secondly their exquisite taste and perfume, qualities which had delightful nuances seemingly allied to the changes in colour; thirdly there was my unforgettable brush with Mother over the cherry tree, which I must now relate.

One year as picking time neared, I decided to see if stolen fruit really was the best, and here Mother caught me truly *in flagrante delicto,* up that old tree gobbling down the fruit, mouth and fingers stained red with guilt. Now I might have thought that her sharp "Come down that tree!" would have sufficed, but Mother (cherry jam in mind?) was out for her pound of flesh, and waited doggedly below with her cane until I tired and slid down to face the music. The question remains unanswered as to whether or not my petty theft had been worth it, but the severe caning I received seemed quite out of proportion to those few cherries.

Here I feel compelled to cite a case of preferential treatment in the matter of fruit stealing within our family. In this instance it concerns gooseberries, a sizeable near-ripe batch having gone missing from a bush in our garden. Naturally I was (wrongly) accused and misbelieved by Mother when I denied this scurrilous allegation! Equally naturally Philip was believed by her when he also denied the charge. However, on this occasion Fate intervened on my behalf in an amusing way, though in fairness the outcome could have been tragic. On that hot summer afternoon Philip was knocked off his cycle by a horse and trap as he wobbled in the narrow lane a short distance from home. They carried him into our cool kitchen, laying him unconscious on the long, scrubbed table. I looked on as they loosened his clothing, worried by the general atmosphere of calamity and his pale face and closed eyes. Suddenly the tension broke for as they carefully turned him on his side his eyes opened and looked at me, and out of his pockets rolled the gooseberries! I laughed with a mixture of relief and the evidence of my vindication, while my parents and the trap driver laughed merely with relief. Philip remained silent, still in the twilight stage between dreams and reality.

Towards the end of growth there is a trick of one-upmanship I would play which stamped a particular fruit as my own, akin to personal numberplates on a car, but not nearly so expensive. The only things required are gummed paper and a pair of scissors, as one's initials applied before final ripening and peeled off when picked result in letters on an apple as clear-cut as bra-marks on a sunbathing beauty's bosom.

Before ripening there would be gatherings of the 'fallings', mostly those apples which had succumbed to the attentions of little nasties curled up inside, revealed either when emerging from their P.O.W.-style escape holes or when the apple was cut open, their black eyes and snub-noses as shiny as healthy young puppies. Yet another of my favourite mind-pictures of Mother shows her coming from one or the other of the orchards, her half-filled apron gathered in front of her, intent on making apple pies from Nature's rejects.

Later falling apples would be gouged out by wasps – not one of my favourite insects, though on the other hand I like most species of bees. Honey bees seldom attack humans unless they or their colonies are threatened, whereas wasps sound, look and act as though they have a permanent chip on their shoulders. Wasp time meant fruit-harvest time, so it would be out with ladders and baskets before those striped bandits spoiled too many apples, pears or plums, in addition to making life difficult for the pickers by their predatory and dog-in-a-manger behaviour.

When as many as possible apples had been gathered pristine and bruise-free from the tree by using ladders, it was time for more-drastic measures to harvest the remainder.

First the outer ones were knocked off with a long clothes prop, followed by the shaking of branches or tree. During this stage it was wise to step back well clear of the tree, as not everyone wishes to rediscover gravity by a painful thump on the head from a free-fall Bramley! Finally there was the stubborn resistance-group to be dealt with, clinging on to the last by the skin of their stalks. They might be dislodged by well-aimed sticks, tennis balls or other handy missiles, and sometimes by the aid of my patent device: this consisted of a large tin can nailed through its base so as to sit on the tip of a long pole, the top of the can having been only part cut away so as to leave a V-shaped cutting edge in which to trap the stalk. As a last resort the Newbound Mill SAS was sent in, as Mother did not object to me climbing fruit trees when it was for the common good.

With all safely gathered in, those apple and pear varieties which would keep were stored on a huge shelf partway up the back stairs, on snug beds of clean straw, the apples protected also by their own coats of wax. There they would rest – some right through to spring – until fetched down for dumplings, tarts, pies, sauce or straightforward eating as dessert.

A favourite occasion of mine for eating apples was while reading boys' magazines or comics on a winter's evening. It became almost a ritual with me to put aside a newly-delivered comic until I had a small stock of apples at my elbow in the little flower basket reserved for them. This meant a trip upstairs to the store, selecting the fruit by candlelight, mindful of the warnings about naked lights and straw. Back downstairs I would sit on my stool by the blazing fire, indulging in the twin pleasures of reading and scrunching my way through the succulent fruits. Sometimes I would be allowed a ripe Conference pear, the uncontrollable flow of juice dripping off my chin onto Billy Bunter, Corky the Cat or somesuch figure from schoolboy fiction.

One victory for me in the ceaseless battle with Philip for smart-lad supremacy came when he bit into a luscious looking apple which I handed to him from the basket, followed by a quick spitting-out of a mouthful of salt. The secret lay in my having previously selected an apple with a blemish which lent itself to concealing a removable trap-door via which I had scooped out a recess into which I crammed the salt. With trap-door pressed back into place, no-one could suspect that this was indeed "a goodly apple with a rotten heart".

Our garden, at the rear of the house, was large enough though not at big as the size of the house would seem to warrant. This presented no problems, as nearby plots in the fields supplemented it for growing some of our domestic requirements. Thus the garden itself was a mixture of vegetables, soft-fruit bushes, flowers and shrubs, having evolved gradually and harmoniously without any apparent planning, which in fact added to its charm. It was bounded by the high stone wall of the house on one side, a view over the old mill roof on the opposite side, a shed at one and a low wall at the other, with steps leading down to the orchard, mill-stream and bridge. The garden was overlooked by the main windows of the house, both from the downstairs rooms and the bedrooms. In all, a pleasantly-mellowed home for plants and the odd wildlife creature alike.

The flowers were pretty much as to be expected in an unsophisticated old-world garden, the names of some of them speaking of romantic though humble origins – foxgloves, canterbury bells, red-hot pokers, forget-me-nots, love-in-a-mist and love-lies-bleeding. Spring would be preceded by her usual heralds – snowdrop, crocus, daffodil and narcissus, whilst in summer tall sunflowers and hollyhocks would peep around the window-edges of kitchen and living-room. The pretty faces of pansies and violas looked up appealingly from borders, sweet peas clung to bamboo canes by their graceful tendrils, delighting the senses with their delicate colours and sweet perfume, while blushing roses remained quietly conscious of their long-established reputation as the emblem of Merry England.

On summer evenings, night-scented stocks gave pleasant reminders of their whereabouts, moths fluttered against softly-lighted windows, swooping bats gave twilight displays of aerobatics, and the resident barn-owl emerged to start his nightly patrol.

Wintry aspects of the garden were of course in general pretty dull, though early on the birds might be glimpsed taking quick snacks of berries from a shrub. They were more in evidence when snow lay on the ground, hanging pitifully around with feathers fluffed out, hoping their cracked old dinner plate might be replenished with scraps from our meal-table. Even when not in sight, the evidence of their footprints remained in the snow, tracing out random patterns or leading to and from their various sheltering places.

The snow was probably far more welcome to us than the birds. I remember one characterful snowman we made in the garden, a cheery soul complete with battered tall hat, scarf and cane. For a couple of days, as viewed mostly from our cosy vantage points inside the house, he seemed to remain unchanged, staring back at us with his cheeky, fixed grin. Then subtly at first but later with increasing acceleration he sank to the ground, his last recognisable shape as a humanoid resembling a particularly dumpy Toulouse Lautrec.

I found that the vegetables grown in our Jack-of-all-trades garden had their own little points of interest to offer. For example, it was difficult to get over the feeling that potatoes actually saw us with those eyes. And did the easily-wounded beetroot feel real pain when we made it bleed by rough handling? Certainly onions possessed the strange power of making us cry when we did not even feel sad or miserable.

With some vegetables there was fun to be had too. As we sat shelling peas, Philip and I would vie with each other as to who could produce the loudest pops, keeping an eye open for Mother so that she did not see how many we ate. The appearance of broad beans amused me, and I would push them just under the toe of my slipper, pretending they were toes with particularly dirty nails. Later in the year came the fashioning of Halloween lanterns from turnips, scooping them out till the wafer-thin shell acted as a globe for the candle to be placed inside, with cut-outs to present grotesque and scary faces.

Other vegetables were quite beautiful in their own way, particularly the marrows, with their variegated stripes in every shade of green and yellow. Kidney-beans brought pleasure by their brilliant red flowers, perfectly set off by the dark-green foliage, and by the attendant bees; the name of my favourite variety rolled majestically off the tongue – Scarlet Emperor.

We grew soft fruits of almost every kind, though with some it was a struggle to preserve enough for ourselves, as the birds also wanted a good share. Strawberries were highly prized by both sides, and what more ambrosial food could we want, especially when straight from the garden, sprinkled with sugar and topped with real cream from our own real cows. At the other end of the taste-scale was the astringent pleasure of eating rhubarb, toned down as required by bland floppings of custard. Pulling those ribbed sticks was one of my minor pleasures, as beneath the canopy of leaves I would sometimes see the toad, squatting like some obese eastern potentate under his cool green palanquin. The few herbs we grew in odd corners gave invitations to indulge in other fleeting sensual moments, and frequently I would pluck a leaf of mint, sage or thyme, merely to savour the perfume released on crushing. New

potatoes with mint, fresh green peas and lamb – what a perfect combination!

Those attractive pictures on seed packets could easily lull the gardener into forgetting the hard work involved before the possibility of achieving similar results. Not that I myself could contribute much help, though there were lowly tasks considered within my capabilities, notably weeding. I learned one lesson early on during my gardening chores, and it still remains almost an obsession with me today – care in putting down a rake. In later life it became apparent what potential danger lay in that innocuous-looking implement, for one step back into it could mean a quick leap forward into eternity. After the particular star-gazing thump I received on the head from a rake-handle, I needed no further warnings in that respect.

As with most old gardens, cultivation was continually unearthing bits and pieces which perpetuated the memories of long-dead former occupants of our house. Fragments of clay pipes, pottery, bottles and ornaments spoke of other times, whilst occasionally the head of a young or old Victoria was revealed when soil was rubbed off a worn coin.

In those days there was not the wide variety of chemical fertilisers, weedkillers, pesticides, fungicides and what-have-yous that so bemuse us today, hence reliance was generally placed on more homely substances. Pre-eminent among fertilizers was that same one as is valued today – farmyard manure, and in our case it was only a short wheelbarrow ride away. You would think that the noble animals had done more than enough towards helping-on the garden in life, yet even when dead and gone their processed bodies were used in the form of dried blood and powdered bone, hoof and horn. Soot from the chimney was used as a soil dressing also, table salt harassed slugs and snails, and various beasts, bugs and blights were discouraged by spraying with used bath water and a nicotine brew concocted from cigarette ends.

On a more romantic note, we children tried our hands at making rose-water, naively merely leaving the petals to steep in a corked bottle for a couple of weeks. The results were certainly odorous, though not quite in the way we had intended. Possibly more successful was the time when my sister steeped herself in the language of flowers. I now understand that, for example, white lilies signify purity, violets denote modesty, and roses stand for love. However, I personally would hesitate to proffer first a red rose ("I love you") followed by a bunch of gladioli ("I am ready armed")!

Finally comes the story of Father and the potato thief. The latter was discovered by my father one evening digging up a whole row of potatoes in an outlying plot, shielded from view by a barn. When challenged, he sized up Father's diminutive size as being of no account, replied with an obscenity and continued stuffing the potatoes into his loot-sack. He had greatly underrated Father, who within seconds had stepped into the barn and reappeared with a loaded shot-gun. The man quickly took to his heels, but by now Father was so incensed that he loosed off both barrels in the general direction of the suddenly terror-stricken spud-snatcher to encourage him on his way. Father had not finished yet, for he hailed the local policeman who chanced to ride by not long afterwards, and the pair of them set out in Father's motor-cycle combination to scour the lanes for the thief. They soon caught up with him and chased him till he tired, the *coup de grace* being administered by the bobby as he leapt from the sidecar onto his quarry. There followed accusation and counter-charge, the thief insisting that Father had shot him up the backside. When asked to drop his trousers and reveal the evidence, he declined on the grounds that it was an affront to his modesty. The affair ended with both sides agreeing to drop the matter. Father's experience of gun-law learned in wild and woolly Canada had won the day.

12

MOUTH-WATERING MEMORIES

With my pen at the ready a few minutes ago to jot down my own contribution to the EEC paper mountain of food literature, it occurred to me that it has all been said before, so what's the use? Picking up yesterday's *Sunday Times* book supplement for confirmation of these proliferations on the subject of 'Food, glorious food!', I find that this applies to four out of the current 'top ten' paperback books and similarly to two out of the 'top five' hardback manuals – which could be either good or bad news for me. However, on reflection I do not expect to be vying in this chapter with the gastronomic experts, as it concerns the more homely recipes or such trivialities as my Uncle George's immense appetite and how the cat got its head fast in a salmon tin and then ran full tilt into the kitchen wall!

Yes, I have mouth-watering memories, and in later years did indeed at times positively yearn for foods and dishes 'just like Mother made it', with one notable exception – cabbage. Here, the kindest thing I can say is that her boiled cabbage *à la maison* might have gained a 'highly commended' in some Blackpool Landladies' cooking competition. Possibly she had read that Vitamin C is concentrated in the stalks and outer leaves and must not be destroyed by overcooking. Not until after I had gone into long trousers did a kindly aunt take me by the hand and lead me back to the cabbage table, with reassurances that all would be well and it did not send young men blind etc. etc.

Mother's forté in the 'greens' line was vegetable broth, best enjoyed when served up piping hot on a raw winter's day. The hands could be warmed by cuddling the white earthenware basin in between spoonfuls of that pale-green herbal brew, with its pungent steam bringing grateful tears to the eyes. Bulk was provided to this tasty concentrate by dropping in small lumps of crusty bread, also used to mop the basin clean, though only after it had been drained by lifting to the lips.

Another memorable dish for a cold day was meat and potato pie, which Mother made to perfection. I can picture Hilda, Philip and myself sitting round as the pie was lifted straight from the oven and over our heads onto the table, the doubled-up oven cloth insulating Mother's hands from the heat of the seething juices trapped inside the volcanic crust. The first-helping portions varied in size according to our ages and appetites, and Mother's "You can start" needed no second invitation, three forks being raised in unison followed by sharp intakes of cooling air to prevent burnt tongues. As each mouthful went down, the remainder in the pie-dish was weighed up to assess our chances of a second helping. If I didn't hurry up Philip might beat me to it with more chance of the lion's share, though with luck he might be off his food today. To prompts of "Get those elbows off the table", we rejoiced in that crumbly pastry and the diced meat and potatoes, each small cube having gained a little flavour from its neighbours. Old King Cole himself could not have had a tastier dish set before him.

Of the cold meats traditional at Newbound Mill Farm, I

can quickly single out rabbit pie for one of the top awards. As I said earlier on, I associate it with Sunday supper-times, particularly on balmy summer evenings. It would have been kept cool on a stone-slabbed shelf in the dairy, and not being over-messy it could be eaten largely with the fingers as the crust was not too crumbly, the bones made for easy handling of the meat and much of the liquid had congealed into a taste-bud-titillating spicy jelly. The pie could be washed down with cold milk as I sat in the kitchen sucking the last bones while Mother moved around in the next room, preparing for her hymn-rendering session at the piano.

One dinner-time custom in our family which most people have found strange was eating yorkshire pudding as a sweet, not instead of but in addition to the times it was served with a roast-beef meat course. In the former role each semi-crisp golden square was half-covered with a dark-red pool of syrupy damson, raspberry or blackberry 'vinegar', and I can recommend this treat to anyone not afraid to stray from the traditional gravy-soaked idea – always provided they have one of the so-called vinegars.

That reference to a strange custom has led me to thinking of the cardboard cylinders of dried peas which were Mother's standby when the garden variety was out of season. Their flavour could scarcely be rated as in the top band of the Gourmet Taste Scale, yet I could never resist picking a few out of their overnight-soak basin for a compulsive chew. The container had its own distinctive though not disagreeable smell, and was welcomed for its model-making potential as I could use it for such things as railway tunnels or artillery mortars.

Returning to foods that follow the main course, I do not particularly care for the word *pudding,* nor do I subscribe fully to the sentiment that 'A rose by any other name would smell as sweet'. My dictionary gives *Pudding:. . . a stiffish mixture . . . enclosed in flour. . . cooked by boiling, steaming. . .* – how dull! On the other hand, *Sweet:. . . tart, cream, jelly. . .* how appetising! A minor hell for me would be a wet washday with a plateful of suet pudding dumped in front of me, whereas there was a foretaste of paradise in blackcurrant tart hotfoot from the baking tin and clothed in fresh cream; eaten cold, it was still delicious and left a moustache of sugar to be licked off.

With cows virtually on the doorstep, it follows that the several varieties of milk pudding featured regularly on our menu, though most of them were not to my own taste. Semolina was too bland, 'frogspawn' (tapioca) too glutinous, whilst rice I could accept as just passable. My favourite was macaroni, as the slender tubes in their raw form could be used for a number of suck-and-blow games, and when cooked I found them palatable and could get further amusement by ingesting them with a rapid suck, causing them to disappear like startled aquatic worms into mudflat boltholes.

To me, a perfect example of a 'just like Mother made it' dish was her apple dumplings. The pastry alone was sufficient to commend them, but the complete ensemble of steaming Bramley apple flesh, clove-flavoured and topped with fresh cream, was indeed food for the gods.

Some of Mother's sweets I could really have gone overboard about, or up to the knees in, were her trifles, presented with pride in the large, cut-glass bowl virtually reserved for those creamy creations. The surface looked bland enough – just a layer of whipped cream scattered with silver cachous and lightly dusted with multi-coloured 'hundreds and thousands'. However, as the large silver spoon scooped and sucked out the first portion, a rich, winey aroma was released and coloured strata were revealed like some exotic archeological excavation. As eating commenced, beatific facial expressions and quiet "Mmms…!" betrayed the subdued gastronomic orgasms in

which the participants were wallowing, and conversation flagged so as to allow full enjoyment of this fleeting rapture.

In continuance of that fruity theme, here let me proclaim "Long live Victoria!" – for she was my plum favourite when freshly picked from our own trees at Newbound Mill, that unique flavour making her the true queen of fruits. Acquaintance would be renewed during the winter when Mother opened one of the large preserving jars fetched downstairs from her storeroom, but like the great queen herself, the bloom of youth had been shed through time, for now the plump, matronly bodies were clothed in Jubilee syrup.

A hint of the tropics entered our house whenever anyone brought home a coconut, with mind-pictures of David Livingstone hacking his way through the jungle as mischievous monkeys aimed nuts at him from lofty palm trees. First we would shake the nut to decide whether or not it contained any of the so-called milk, to be released by piercing one of the eyes with a six-inch nail. I believe that when Philip and I drank that insipid liquid it merely satisfied imaginings that we were thirst-crazed explorers, saved from death by a timely discovery of the nut in a clearing. The flesh was more-truly prized, perhaps because it resisted all but the most determined assaults on the nut to get at it, finally yielding when Frank or Father shattered it with a large hammer.

Cakes were some of Mother's specialities, my particular memories being of her cream-filled sponges and chocolate sandwiches, with date-and-walnut or cherry cakes as close runners-up. Her six-foot-six brother George loved to gorge himself on those confections, and once had the laugh on her when she cut a thin slice from a cake and then offered him the remainder as a joke – he ate the lot! They would tell the story of how, as teenagers, they ate part of a cake produced for a birthday, then panicked as they realised the implications. (Their mother was that stern old grandmother of mine). The day was saved by Uncle George making a suitable wedge of wood, inserted and iced over by Mother, the cake eventually being positioned carefully on the birthday table so that the bogus segment faced away from their dour-faced presiding mother. There was a further scare when someone turned the cakestand around to admire the decorations, but the situation was restored by more appreciations and turnings by Mother.

The open fire made it possible to enjoy treats like hot buttered toast or pikelets, with pleasure in the preparation as well as the eating. Seated well back on a low stool so as to avoid being scorched by the roasting-hot fire, we would cautiously advance the long toasting-fork until the impaled slice began to sizzle and smoke, with frequent inspections to ensure just the right degree of crispy browning. Hilda would sometimes find herself hearthbound in her attempts to keep up with the greedy-chick demands of her two young brothers.

In what for our family were those less-affluent, unsophisticated days, we drank far more of that commonest of commodities – water, or else tea and milk. Purchased soft drinks were considered a special treat, to be enjoyed only on trips to town or on high days and holidays. In particular, I have in mind the various mineral waters sold in those marble-stoppered bottles so much favoured by present-day collectors of this category of nostalgia-steeped item. The contents went by names like dandelion-and-burdock, cream soda and sarsaparilla; they were so fizzy that inavoidable burping sent back-pressure gusts of slightly painful gas bubbles down our tender young nostrils.

One year, Mother's attempts to brew ginger beer as a harvest-field refreshment displayed an uncharacteristic lack of know-how on her part. Her premature bottling of the stuff and tightening of the screwed stoppers resulted in a series of frightening explosions during the night; morning investigations revealed a pantry with walls and ceilings soaked in the frothy beverage while glass fragments lay embedded in the whitewashed plaster and scattered around shelves and floor. Come to think of it, of course Mother was not familiar with the promiscuous and prolonged breeding habits of yeast cells – she was teetotal!

Finally in this recital of food memories come those home-made sweets which rivalled the shop-bought gob-stoppers, striped humbugs, sherbet suckers, aniseed balls, lemon drops and so on. Shallow baking trays served as moulds for Mother's mixes of chocolate fudge, treacle toffee or butterscotch. I preferred the hard varieties, first prised from the tray and then hammered into mouth-sized pieces using the heavy nutcrackers, with tiny splinters sticking to our eager hands and faces.

That would seem to have licked the plate of this subject fairly clean.

13

LESSONS FROM BOOK AND BIBLE

To receive my secular and spiritual enlightment involved a great deal of walking, as Teversal school and church lay nearly two miles from home, and there was no school bus, and no bicycle to ride. On the way I would call at a cottage for my friend Leonard. His father worked on a nearby farm and was generally taking a short break after breakfast when I arrived. It was interesting to meet him as not only was he jolly but he let me enjoy the thrill of handling several Roman coins found during his earlier days as a ploughman in Lincolnshire. Len's account of these finds led me to believe that the fields there were littered with coins, simply awaiting picking up.

Sometimes I would have to wait a short while until Len was ready, as it was a busy time for his mother, what with breakfast to prepare, Len's sandwiches to pack and a new baby clamouring for attention. This meant we would have to trot most of the way to school, listening in the hope that the bell would not ring before we got there.

The school stood on the very edge of our side of the little village, up a short rise in the ground. It looked much as many other Victorian village church schools, brick-built and surrounded by a small playground, the whole enclosed by iron railings. Few as we pupils were (around forty in all), the two high-ceilinged classrooms were stretched to their capacity, and the three female teachers must also have been working at their limits. It was not so much the number of children each had under her care as the range of ages and the problems of more than one class sharing the same small room. There was a folding partition between the rooms for infants and older children, but this only went part-way to alleviating that noisy situation. Part-way is also appropriate for describing how the cast-iron stove coped with heating the classroom on cold winter days. It would be stoked up with coke from an iron bin until the tortoise emblem on the lid grew red in the face, as did the pupils nearest to it, while those in the back row still felt cold.

My first next-door neighbour in our semi-detached desks was Pat, who I still remember with affection. She was rather shy, good-natured, slim, fair and pretty. During our self-introductions we discovered that she was 'seven on the eighth' whilst I was 'eight on the ninth' (of August), a seemingly inconsequential fact which neither of us forgot. I was fond also of Pat's older sister Sylvia, though she was the opposite of Pat in several respects, being darker, shorter, very active and forceful, but attractive. I make particular mention of those two sisters as, extraordinarily, they were to re-enter my life many years later – in effect an acquaintance-void stretching from school-slate days to our lap-size personal computer era.

Each morning started with prayers ("Our Father 'chart in 'eaven. . . ") followed by the handing-out of pens and pencils, books and paper, and then we were settled down for lessons. Few of us could have appreciated that we were in the process of being given, and shown how to use, the basic tools for going about the various lives that lay ahead of us.

Personally I believe that one of the biggest factors in how we get on at school is our relationship with our teachers, for a lack of rapport between us must spell trouble from the very start. Here I consider myself lucky, for I do not recall any particular conflict with the school mistresses at Teversal. I remember little of the infants' teacher, Mrs Parsons, other than her wireless-coil hair-style, as I was soon transferred to the main room under Miss Harpham who was at the 'flapper' age, and would sometimes be whisked away on the pillion of a motorcycle when school ended. The headmistress, Miss Clarke, was of a much maturer age, tall and stately, and wore long dresses which almost swept the classroom floor. She appeared to glide across the ground, like one of those impassive and apparently legless members of a Caucasian dance troupe. I found her sympathetic, but then book-learning came fairly easily to me, so I was of no trouble to her in that respect, hence I was seldom reprimanded or physically punished. Not that I remember the cane being used a great deal, though it sometimes lay threateningly on her desk. I can, however, picture a few clashes between her and a tubby boy named Colin. As a stern-faced Miss Clarke brandished her cane over Colin's outstretched hand, a short duel of wits would commence. There would be a short sizing-up of each other followed by a rapid swish-snatch, swish-snatch – pause – swish-Ouch! Victory to Miss Clarke, as eventually she sold Colin the dummy!

Around the classroom on walls and shelves were all the trappings and adjuncts to learning of a typical old-time village school. An oilcloth map highlighted the British Empire in proud red patches whilst a globe proved that Australia really was down under; Moses gazed awestruck at the burning bush; jam jars of frogspawn served as a lead-in to sex (Nature, as it was called), and pinned-up all around were examples of good work by industrious little creeps, anxious to please teacher.

The hubbub and general distractions of more than class made it difficult to concentrate at times, except during joint activities such as reciting our 'times tables'; some disinterested scholars seemed scarcely to progress further than the 'One one is one, two ones are two' stage, though doubtless most of them learned how many pints in a quart not too long after leaving school.

Although I was a messy writer, literally blotting my copybook and also crossing my pen-nibs more than most of my classmates, I loved English lessons, particularly composition. One morning we sensed by Miss Clarke's smiling demeanour and opening remarks that she had something special to tell us all. Finally she came out with it, announcing that a story of mine (about gangsters using a haunted castle as a hideout) had been published in the magazine *Teachers' World*. I had arrived! With one arm outstretched theatrically, she pointed at me and pronounced "That boy will write books!" Apart from basking in the seven-day-wonder atmosphere of it all, I benefited by receiving from her a suitably inscribed book as a reward. To add further to my elation at that time, a similar composition by my rival – brother Philip – attracted ridicule by his opening line which read "Stealthy footsteps were heard under the bed." I needled him by suggesting that the noise probably emanated from a dwarf, looking for the chamber-pot.

History stirred my imagination too. I can sympathise with those who were put off this subject for life by the dreary chore of date-memorising, but I managed to overcome this, helped a great deal by the pictures in our dog-eared primers. Some were as vivid as if 'our correspondent at Hastings' had whipped out his pocket Leica to capture some of those historic events on the spot. There stood Harold, shaken a little but still attempting to pluck the arrow from his eye as though it were some irritating splinter; turn back a few pages and the arrogant Canute sat crowned and enthroned at the edge of the advancing surf. (Late extra: 'Crackpot Monarch Angered by Sea's Defiance').

There were occasional breaks from the blackboard-and-easel dominated room, such as nature walks, welcomed more for the social pleasures of our crocodile-stroll down the lane than for any real instruction on the flora and fauna around us. We probably learned more about each other than of the birds and bees!

There was one subject at which that backwater little school excelled, and for which it gained a reputation throughout the area – singing. We knew we were good, as we were constantly reminded of our prowess by the embroidered silk and satin banners which hung around the classroom walls, the trophies of our successes at music festivals in Mansfield, Retford, Worksop and Nottingham. This was of course all thanks to Miss Clarke's love of music and her talent for passing it on to us and training us. We bathed in the sweet sentiment of the *Londonderry Air,* gave solemnly subdued renderings of *Our Blest Redeemer,* and relished the jolly singing of "Come lasses and lads, get leave of your dads, and away to the maypole hie."

Visits to those music festivals were eagerly-anticipated days out for us, our little team of around a dozen travelling there in a small private bus, all rigged out in our Sunday-best. At the Nottingham festival, we found ourselves in a long queue along a side-street, awaiting admission to the Albert Hall along with other school choirs. The boredom of waiting meant that my streak of mischief needed only the flimsiest excuse for any airing, and there it was on a corner – a joke-shop. Now irresponsible as what followed may seem, after all it is the stuff of youth, so I will continue my story. After studying the tricks on offer, I selected itching-powder, and whispered my intentions of disabling the rival choirs by the use of this (as I now realise) noisome preparation. Pinches of it were surreptitiously dropped down the necks of several would-be young Carusos, and the resultant discomfort was soon apparent. However, it transpired that I was pinpointed as the culprit, and retaliation followed by the cutting-off of both my braces buttons at the rear. As a result, I was the only ill-bred, insolent and red-faced brat to stand on the platform singing "Come lasses and lads . . . " with both hands in trousers pockets, Miss Clarke was not amused.

Our morning and afternoon breaks from lessons were spent in the fairly confined area of the playground, so fights were not uncommon. Here I learned early on that bullies are often not as tough as they may wish to be seen, relying largely on intimidation and generally backing down when the worm turns. Other playtime lessons learned were to be alert on dates such as April Fools' Day and Oak Apple Day. On the latter occasion, failure to wear a sprig of oak leaves (which had to include an oak-apple) to commemorate Charles II's escape up an oak tree incurred the penalty of being well and truly stung by bunches of nettles.

One sunny playtime as we stood in line awaiting being filed back into school, our shadows on the ground fell in such a way as to suggest a naughty joke too good to be missed. Selecting a sensitive type of victim, by hand manipulations I added to his natural shadow in a place which embarrassed him most, to the great amusement of all the others, including the girls in the back row. Squirm in embarrassment as he may, that alien protuberance stuck to his own shadow like glue, until even he was forced to laugh. There was nothing easier than to remove the evidence when Miss Harpham approached to investigate.

Miss Clarke introduced piano accompaniments to brighten

up those return-to-classroom occasions, such as marching in to the tune of *Colonel Bogey.* That proved to be an unfortunate choice for her, as some boy enlightened us as to the words used at the Miners' Club, which start with "Don't throw the lamp at father. . . ." Dear Miss Clarke did not move in such circles, so was puzzled at the uncontrollable hilarity which the tune always sparked off. (Equally puzzled readers will not find the answer in the *Oxford Dictionary of Quotations*!)

Possibly half the pupils could reach home for the midday meal break, the rest of us remaining to eat our sandwiches where we may, as the days of school dinners lay very much in the future. On cold winter days this was not much fun at all, as we would be cooped up in the classroom, not daring to stand too close to the stove unless invited by Miss Clarke.

Better weather meant better things to do, much of it in the nearby fields, the farmers not making too much fuss providing we respected crops and livestock. A friend Richard and I would hunt for edible corms we called pig-nuts. First we would track down the plant by its tell-tale long, slender stem and crown of florets, then dig down to unearth the crunchy, nutty-flavoured snack. Naturally we would climb trees, and just as naturally tore jerseys and trousers in the process, limping back with sprained ankles and cut knees.

One dinner-time, keen to show my skills acquired from dabbling with my chemistry outfit, I announced my plan to exterminate the wasps which had been harassing our school community from a nest in the adjoining field – chemical warfare. I knew that burning sulphur produced a knock-out gas, and assured my henchmen that a small pile lit outside the entrance of the nest would produce quick results – it did! No sooner had match touched powder than the nest spat a succession of yellow buzz-bombs at me, zapping me like ground-to-air missiles. I fled pell-mell, all thoughts of glory gone as they homed-in on hands, face and knees till I really felt my end had come – the biter well and truly bit!

On days when our headmistress had been home at midday, the approaching end of dinner-time would be signalled by relayed murmurings of "Miss Clarke's coming!" She had a straight, 150-yard processional walk from her garden gate to the school entrance, her progress having indeed an air of royalty about it. The regal atmosphere was often enhanced by a small group of fawning young courtiers who ran to greet her, seeking to ingratiate themselves by bright-eyed chatterings along the last half of her stage-entrance walk.

A dinner-time prank of mine which misfired entailed hiding in the bottom compartment of a book cupboard in the cloakroom, so as to surprise the monitoress, Sylvia, when she opened it at the start of lesson-time. I was such a tight fit in there that, even crouched up like a trussed chicken, my accomplice Len had literally to force my last bits in, and to say that it was uncomfortable is a gross understatement. Things went wrong: firstly Sylvia did not come for books as expected, and secondly as time wore on and I tried to get out, I found I could move neither limb nor muscle, and I became rather frightened. Meanwhile, Miss Clarke had been fobbed off as to my whereabouts, but later became suspicious and grilled Len into a confession. She was led to the scene of my voluntary incarceration, and by a painful Houdini-in-reverse exercise, eventually I was extracted. It says much for Miss Clarke's tolerance of me that I received nothing worse than a telling off. (I believe that secretly she was more than mildly amused!).

The afternoons would wear on, completing each of those days of our education which were to play a part in turning out a generous share of minor achievements for that little school. They also helped shape the lives of all of us who sat at those ink-stained desks – demure-looking little angels and embryo young scoundrels alike. Finally the last bell of the day would sound, and for me this meant the start of my long walk back.

Those walks home, often with my travelling companion Len, brought temptations to enliven the journey with boyish tomfoolery, but here I would like to relate a story which highlights the dangers of circumstantial evidence. My tale starts on a hot sunny afternoon during corn harvest time, when Len and I had so dawdled on the first part of our way home that we were overtaken by one of our classmates, René. Her father's farmstead lay in the centre of the village, but she was on her way to the harvest field with the men's tea-time meal, the contents of the large basket on her arm being covered with a spotless-white damp cloth, as was the practice. After a few boy-girl pleasantries, we noticed that she also carried a spare ball of binder-twine for the horse-drawn reaping machine; in high spirits we grabbed the twine from her and bowled it down the hill so that several yards of it unreeled. This was not a particularly helpful thing to do, either for René or for whoever had to sort things out before fitting the ball to the sheaf-binding mechanism, so when her father subsequently gave us the rough edge of his tongue, we took this as even less than we deserved. And there, for the moment, the story rests.

At school a few days later, Len and I were puzzled when Miss Clarke called us out into the cloakroom, where we were confronted by the local policeman. To our astonishment, he accused us both of taking our revenge for the dressing-down by cutting the string around every single sheaf of corn in the field which had been reaped on the day of our horseplay with the ball of twine. We were in fact totally innocent in that respect, but by persistent and unrelenting third-degree tactics that zealous bobby finally reduced us to tears of exasperation and a false admission of the crime. Fortunately my father straightway took the matter up, and I shall always be grateful to him for standing up for me and averring that although I was mischievous he had never caught me out in a lie. The matter was dropped. Now I am, and always have been a staunch supporter of the principles of law and order, but for me that affair tainted my image of policemen for life. Ever since then, any mention of third-degree immediately evokes my sympathy for anyone who has been subjected to it; after all, were were only boys of eleven.

Perversely enough, a few pleasanter memories of those journies home from school concern much worse weather but a far more sympathetic man – the baker. On several occasions Len and I would be hurrying along either cold, wet or both when the welcome sound of the approaching baker's van spelt relief. That kindly man would stop, invite us up beside him and give us a warm, freshly-baked currant bun to eat. Bliss! We would jog along protected from the weather by the hood, swaying against each other as the wheels struck stones or ruts, savouring the sweet buns like manna fallen from the most unpromising looking of heavens. The creak of van springs, squeal of iron tyres and clip-clop of hooves combined to form a pastoral symphony, the spasmodic bass element being supplied by the horse breaking wind in bursts of toccata or drawn-out sustained notes.

The religious part of my education involved the same long walk from Newbound Mill Farm to Teversal village, though in good weather the second part of the journey could be shortened via pleasant footpaths across the fields. This route eventually finished up near the church itself, a medieval building, small but full of character, pushed to the very edge of the village by the centuries-long vagaries of shifting social patterns and requirements.

Alongside the church stood the rambling and spacious eighteenth-century vicarage, built in the days when many clerics prized such retreats either for indulging in hunting and port drinking with the squire, or for burying themselves in such academic pursuits as studying the local fauna and

BAKER

flora – or for all we know Faith and Charity! In my time it housed the Revd George Eaton, a likeable, mild-mannered and bespectacled bachelor, though said to be fond of female company. Miss Clarke appeared to entertain aspirations in his direction, though the prize was not to fall in her lap – nor she in his!

Mr Eaton was best-known to us for his periodic visits to school for checks on our progress in scripture lessons there, but as members of the church choir Philip and I met him during Sunday morning services also. Philip was a bad influence on me in that choir, and I can recall two occasions in particular when he brought down on my head the odium of the local dignitaries in the congregation for uncontrollable giggling. First he amended one line of a psalm to "Put thy ears into thy bottle"; next came the question of plumbing noises from the vestry, Philip insisting that the trickling of water heard now and again was in fact the vicar relieving himself out there. Again it was the mental imagery that was my undoing, for the thought of our vicar fumbling among his vestments proved just too much for me!

In the afternoons I would make that trip across the fields all over again to attend Sunday-school, which was as much a social occasion as of any value in my religious upbringing. In any case, attendance meant one more coloured stamp in my book, showing biblical scenes with semitic figures immaculately clad in robes of such Persil-like whiteness as I seldom came across in real life during my Middle-East travels in later years.

I must have learned something, at Sunday-school for I still treasure a book prize inscribed "For telling the story of the Good Samaritan so nicely". Those words still give me a twinge of conscience, for they infer a well-scrubbed, brilliantine-haired little Sunday-school angel which rather belies the true facts.

However, I did in fact make myself useful from time to

time at Sunday-school, by blowing the organ for Miss Hartshorne. When she used full swell it was as much as my puny arms could cope with, as I stretched on tiptoes to pump the handle like mad, trying to keep the dangling lead indicator-weight between the two marks scribed in the polished wood by some long-dead craftsman. The sharp-featured Polly Hartshorne seemed to take a sadistic delight in pulling out lots of those ivory-faced stops when I was the duty pumping lad.

Our little class would sometimes stand in the small organ-loft, and I remember one day enjoying a pleasant spell of flirtation with a girl through eye contact and smiles via the organist's mirror, but to no avail. She had been leading me on, for tentative face-to-face advances later on bore no fruit.

The scarcity of pupils of the right age for bible-class resulted in me being press-ganged into the group a little younger than was usual. My only vague memories of those times are of us sitting sedately in the vicar's drawingroom on a lovely summer afternoon, the french windows propped open with a fascinating animal-shaped door-stop. The vicar beamed benignly at us over the top of his nose-perched spectacles and offered us the benefits of clergy from a box of chocolates. All was sweetness and light.

The subject of religion brings to mind the spiritual experience of the young twins Beatrice and Winifred, who insist that they saw an angel on their way home. Len and I would pass the spot concerned when we took the footpath across the fields, and I would always be touched by a feeling of awe as we neared that place. Personally I only ever encountered a barn owl making a daytime sortie around that area, his outstretched wings not unlike those of the angels depicted in Victorian paintings of religious subjects.

And so endeth the thirteenth lesson.

14

GETTING OUT AND ABOUT

Much as I loved my home life, my family and the animals, yet it was refreshing to get away at times on errands, local visits, or best of all on real holidays.

No buses ran within two miles of our home nor did even a carrier's cart, so we depended on our own primitive forms of transport, ranging upwards from Shanks' pony through the horse and trap to Father's Triumph motorbike and sidecar.

Walking never struck us as a particular hardship; after all, we did four miles each day simply going to and from school or church, so another four to Pleasley and back on shopping errands was mere routine. No wonder poor old Father could often be heard cobbling away at the family's footwear at night. At least walking gave us plenty of time to look around us and take in something of what affected other people and forms of life, instead of dashing about selfishly as we do today – heedless of anyone's comfort or way of life except our own. We did not even have a cycle between us to make us speed-crazy like the townies!

The horse and trap was powered by our chestnut Gilbert who was described as 'half-legged', indicating that he could either lumber along pulling a plough or trot smartly between the light shafts of his master's runabout vehicle. What a thoroughly pleasant form of transport that was, from the moment when it tilted against the springs on stepping up via the footplate, to journey's end when Gilbert gave a prolonged snort and looked round for the anticipated nosebag full of oats. Clip-clop clippity-clop down the green lanes, brushing under leafy branches and past tall grasses, perched up with a good view across hedges and walls to where sheep and cattle paused from their grazing to stare in semi-interest at us as we passed by on our carefree way. Even at night there was a touch of romance about those trips, with the rush of cool air and the mellow light of the candle-lamps. Those lamps gave insufficient light to really assist the driver, serving more as markers to help the occasional pedestrian who would step onto the verge till we had gone by, wishing us a friendly "Goodnight" as we passed on into the dark.

Our motorbike and sidecar gave us status – a progressive family though somewhat below the horseless carriage fraternity. After a few kick-start splutterings and explosions we were on our way, Father half-crouched against the wind with his flat cap back-to-front, Mother huddled down behind the cracked celluloid windscreen of the sidecar, and myself seated on the pillion, clinging firmly onto Father's belted coat. I was always being pulled up for leaning the wrong way as we cornered, as those frightening one-and-a-half-G turns were experiences outside the normal range of country travel. The motorbike's illumination was also one-up on that of the horse and trap, consisting of carbide lamps, fuelled by stinking, chalk-like lumps activated by drips of water from a small reservoir on the top. It was not unknown for users of these devices to take fright when they flared out of control, abandoning their vehicles and running for dear life! One winter's night during a period of extraordinarily hard frost, we were on our way home from a visit when the lamp petered out through lack of water. There being not a single drop to be found even after cracking the ice in a roadside ditch, I was called on to oblige, as Father believed that the alcohol from the glass of beer provided by his host might produce an adverse chemical reaction from those capricious lumps of fuel if he were the donor himself.

To me, the most familiar forms of public transport during those mid-1920s years were the tramcars on the Pleasley to Mansfield route. As I pause at this moment, I find it easy to recall and enjoy the sights and sounds of those apparently wheel-less sheds gliding along their shiny rails which snaked down the main streets. A short wait generally brought the next one along, its peculiar low, grinding whine heard way before it appeared around some distant bend, rising and falling in pitch as the tram accelerated or came to rest. A strident clanging of the bell warned other road users of the leviathan's approach, while the hiss of small pulleys along the overhead cables was frequently interrupted by the crack and splutter of brilliant blue sparks. Whether in the enclosed downstairs part or sitting aloft in the open, there were games to be played based on ticket numbers, with the constant change of passengers providing plenty of additional interest.

Even more adventurous for we children was travelling by rail, usually on holidays or day trips of some kind. Important as our tickets made us feel, nearly all of the other people waiting on the platform seemed to have the sophisticated air of seasoned travellers, setting them apart from we country peasants. Some strolled slowly up and down with the measured tread of men born to command; fur-coated ladies stood arrogantly by expensive looking luggage; and family groups sat around reading magazines, chatting or consulting watches. Occasionally someone would press a coin into one of the solidly constructed slot machines, extracting thin bars of milk chocolate with a confident flick-flack of the dispensing tray, as though to the manner born. These were obviously men of the world, with knowledge and skills beyond the ken of simple folk like ourselves – or were they, for suddenly one of them addresses Mother hesitantly: "Excuse me, but is this the right platform for Nottingham?" An idol with feet of clay! With renewal confidence in our own clan, we climb aboard when the train steams slowly in to a halt. Soon, after a succession of slammed doors and shouted commands, a whistle sounds and yes – we really are on the move! There are rules to be learned: don't lean out of windows (cinders), close them when a long whistle warns of a tunnel (suffocating smoke), and don't put your feet up on the seats (manners!), but we soon get the hang of things and begin to enjoy ourselves.

With any luck the walls of the railway carriage would be panelled with advertisements, chiefly lauding the attractions of various holiday resorts. There were the ubiquitous ones such as the Kyle of Lochalsh or Gleneagles, smacking of highland cattle and tam-o-shantered Scotsmen. More homely to our English eyes was the jolly, overweight fisherman, bouncing along in his sou'wester like a human medicine-ball to remind us that 'Skegness is so bracing!'; or we could spend five minutes gazing at an invitation to make a reduced-fare visit to see the Blackpool Illuminations – all the fairyland jewellery of those coloured lights reflected in the sea!

There was fun to be had (though not with Mother present!) from smacking the cushioned seats, as in those pre vacuum-cleaner days you could guarantee to raise a satisfying cloud of fine dust. With no disrespect to the cleaners, those seats were not ideally suited for young ladies in white party dresses. Care had to be taken also when touching the undersides of armrests and seats, as some previous traveller may have parked his masticated-to-death chewing gum there.

The arrival at our destination would be confirmed by platform staff shouting the name of the station, while the engine stood blowing off steam, and there were helpful porters in attendance, spurred on no doubt by visions of a tip for humping luggage around.

I should mention briefly that other form of transport still very much in its infancy at the time – aviation. A single memory of it remains with me, as one day an aeroplane flew close enough to Teversal school for us to shout excitedly to one another – "Look, you can see the man in it!"

Back to the more mundane level of our own horizon, for the neighbours on our visiting list could be counted on the fingers of one hand, but seeing them was no less welcome for that. Nearest to us were the Wraggs up over the hill, where teenagers Annie and Elizabeth would make such a fuss over me that I became embarrassed, feeling a beetroot-red blush spread to the very tips of my ears. There seemed to to be girls everywhere, for at the Renshaws I would hope to see the shyly attractive Betty, while further afield there was Molly Carver with the swan-like elegance of her gentle and charming mother. When I mention our landlord, bluff Mr Heathcote, and the Chambers family who included three of my school companions, then that covers them all.

Mother took us on odd day-trips to Nottingham, where one treat was a pleasure-steamer trip down the river from Trent Bridge to Colwick Weir. With luck I could just manage to trail my hand in the water, lulled by the steady beat of the engine and savouring the tangy reed-cum-fish smell of the river. We would disembark for half an hour at the riverside tea-gardens, where there was unpalatable stewed tea to drink, this penalty being offset by the toothsome fancy pastries set out on the tables under the trees.

Cheap day excursions to Skegness were another diversion, jostling on and off packed trains amid a crush of distracted mums and howling infants. There was always someone kicking up a hullabaloo over a lost bucket and spade or because he had still got sand in his eyes. On the beach, blowsy matrons displayed revolting fat bums as they tucked summer frocks inside their bloomers prior to paddling in the surf, while their beer-and-winkles sated husbands snored in deck-chairs, balding pates protected from sunburn by the obligatory knotted handkerchiefs. For us, there were rides on lovable but sad-eyed and smelly donkeys, velvet-lick ice-cream cornets, sand-castles, Punch & Judy shows, whirligig roundabouts and five-minute friendships – in fact all the fun and excitement of a typically English 'I do like to be beside the seaside' day out.

Two or three holidays which still bring back the pleasantest of memories were those I spent with my cousins Jack and Nancy at Birmingham, a brash city in complete contrast to our homely rural environment, but full of new thrills. We spent arc-lit evenings at the greyhound-racing stadium, or watching leather-clad speedway stars like 'Sprouts' Elder perform feats of derring-do on the cinder track at Perry Bar. Nancy and I were well matched in our vivacity and mischievous sense of fun, and at afternoon swimming sessions the indoor baths would ring with the echoes peculiar to such places as we chased and fooled around in and out of the chlorinated water. Just as lively were the cinema matinées (in this case, children's rowdy

free-for-alls), with harassed operators trying to bring the unruly young mob to order before starting the show. There was the crunch of monkey-nut shells underfoot and the pungent smell of orange peel everywhere, with lads and lasses climbing onto seats and waving noisy greetings to friends across the hall.

Finally I would here like to pay tribute to dear old Granny Draycott by a brief reference to a holiday Philip and I spent at her cottage in Normanton-on-Soar, Leicestershire. She was the sweetest and jolliest of grandmas anyone could wish for, and during the time in question she organised races between we rival brothers, the prizes being lumps of sugar which we strived for as keenly as if they were Olympic gold medals. God rest that kindliest of souls.

15

FUN AND RELAXATION

On the question of occupying our leisure hours, I feel that at Newbound Mill we were quite well favoured both in respect of where we lived and when we lived: there was no artificial entertainment on our doorstep and the seductions of television had not yet arrived to keep us moronically hearthbound. In addition, during those formative years I developed the ability to sidestep the slightest risk of boredom by making good use of whatever facilities and materials lay to hand, coupled with a little imagination, and that talent has served me well throughout my life.

Although many of my spare time activities were pursued on a solitary basis, a few were in essence simply competitions with Philip. One of these pleasures was our annual Boat Race, which took place in an atmosphere of deadly earnest around the same time as the national event. The requirements were simple – two sticks, the stream and our innate rivalry. From the outset we were content that Philip should be Oxford and myself Cambridge, and that is how I came to support the Light Blues to this day! In preparation for our contest a stretch of 'river' would be cleared of weeds and other obstructions, but there were still the inevitable jams and snags, resulting in arguments leading to grabbed jerseys, hair pulling and kicked shins. So keenly was the competition felt that it came to be reflected in our reactions to the results of the real event, and when Cambridge lost I would take Philip's taunts as a personal affront.

Cigarette cards provided scope for other forms of competition and disputes, though with slightly less aggression than the Boat Races. The first problem was one of supply, as the only smokers in our immediate circle were Father and Frank, so Philip and I tried to extract promises from them re the next card and would keep a close check on how many cigarettes they smoked. Primarily the cards were collected for the challenge of making up a complete set – *Kings and Queens of England, Cricketers, Butterflies, Cries of London, Flags of all Nations* – there was a range of these colourful, beautifully produced and informative miniatures which no schoolboy of those times could ever forget. A lively trade existed in swapping the cards or bartering them for other commodities such as conkers or coloured marbles; these transactions could be spotted some distance away by characteristic delvings into jerseys for the carefully wrapped merchandise.

A very popular game with cigarette cards was the test of who could flick one the farthest, with 'winner takes all' as the prize. Here there were considerations not only of dexterity and gauging the wind etc., but also which of your cards you were prepared to risk against the opposing ones as viewed; although newer cards were aerodynamically superior, each flight and landing reduced their efficiency, whilst the grubby cards put up in opposition may not have been worth competing for. Similar in skill was the bouncing of thin stones across stretches of smooth water, the mill-pond being our obvious practice ground. The winner was he who achieved the most clear bounces (room for controversy again!).

Playing at conkers was very much a boys' game, perhaps partly because the hardened, wrinkled nuts were unlikely to attract much girlish attention, but probably more due to the likelihood of receiving some very painful whacks on the fingernails while playing the game itself. The fun began with gathering the nuts in autumn and then subjecting them to various methods of seasoning and toughening-up, including pickling and hanging up the chimney for weeks on end. During the season, as each fight to the death ended in the winner smashing his opponent's nut completely off its string, the conquering nut had one added to its score (plus any victories already credited to the losing nut). Thus a nut could be a 'oner', 'fiver', 'twenty-fiver' or whatever, and their pedigrees and fame soon became known as their owners sought further bouts with challengers of comparable status.

Another profit-or-loss pastime was playing at marbles, with plenty of expertise involved in the different variants of the game, though they all boiled down to skill in hitting rival pieces. Undoubtedly much of the attraction lay also in the colours of the plain and variegated marbles themselves, and the miser-like pleasure of running one's fingers through a linen bagful of them. And whatever happened to the game called 'snobs', all that tossing into the air of dice-like cubes, snatching some off the ground before the rest were caught, in changing patterns calling for a deftness akin to that of a professional juggler.

It was while we lived at Newbound Mill that I learned to swim, partly in the Mansfield swimming baths and sometimes in a local river. In the years to come I was to be thankful that I had persevered in that self-taught art, for it not only proved useful but was a frequent source of pleasure, both at home and abroad. In the early stages my confidence was buoyed up (!) by the use of inflatable 'water wings', and I graduated from a simple dog-paddle style to some semblance of a crawl. And I could even beat Philip!

My youthful dabblings in aeronautical engineering were not attended by even the modest success I achieved later under RAF tuition, but then the early pioneers of this black science were more notorious for their pathetic failures than renowned for solid achievements. I now see clearly that I had failed to grasp the basic precept that the term heavier than air did not mean limitlessly-heavier than air, for both my kites with hazel-branch structures and my hot-air balloons using flour-paste as an adhesive failed miserably to rise to my expectations (those puns again!). My imagination had been kindled by reading of Montgolfier's airborne gondola carrying aloft a crew of cock, goat and sheep, but my dreams of even a lone hen getting her birdseye view of our haystacks were shortlived, and in any case Father had expressed grave concern about spirit-soaked wads of flaming cotton-wool floating over the stackyard.

That range of self-amusements loosely grouped under the heading of hobbies never really appealed to me personally, because it smacked too much of repetition whereas as I favoured variety and breaking new ground. However, I admired the results produced by my cousin Tom with his fretwork kit: there were pipe-racks, egg-racks, letter-racks and ornament-racks, but then what happened when the captive market of relatives had been saturated with these white elephants? Presumably boredom would set in – unless sufficient people were spineless enough to accept more pipe-racks, egg-racks. . . (pardon me, but I just nodded off!).

A project of mine which proved to bring more pleasure in the anticipation than the realisation was the purchase of a South American tree-frog through an advert in a boys' magazine. I spent a great deal of time in converting an upended orange box into a two-storey maisonette for this exotic, sucker-footed croaker, providing a thick, floor-to-roof branch so that Pedro could enjoy either the ground floor or bedroom vista as the whim might seize him. The result? – nothing but lingering fantasies, for stocks of the rugby-jersey clad beast were exhausted before my five-shilling order could be met.

The gentle diversion of blowing bubbles could still be enjoyed using clay pipes, as these were smoked by sufficient country folk as to make them readily available. The fragile, soap and glycerine globes would set me marvelling as to how it was that I could produce them so easily, always perfectly shaped and each with its rainbow-coloured pictures of the kitchen windows. Like all our dreamy creations, they did not stand up well to the realities of life, vanishing at a touch to leave only a light sprinkle of fairy dew on the face.

As each autumn approached I would keep an eye open for the first fireworks to appear on display in a certain shop window in Pleasley. I was simply obsessed with the things ever since being given the chemistry outfit, having experimented with making various coloured fires, smokes and spurtings. I would continually re-read the labels on the small stock which I accumulated with my Saturday's earnings, enjoying in my mind's eye the unspectacular pleasures of fairy lights and sparklers, the multi-coloured whirlings of catherine wheels, the breathtaking express-train rushes of skyrockets, the capricious, firecracking leaps of jumping-jacks, and the sudden, over-loud fright of bangers. Sometimes the real Firework Night was not as exciting as the imagined one!

There was another bang-producing toy popular at that time which I am sure would not comply with today's safety standards. It was a thumb-sized aerial bomb made of cast iron, in two halves to permit the insertion of an explosive cap. The user would whirl it around by its string then fling it high into the air, with or without a shouted warning of "Take cover!" God help anyone who might have received a direct hit on the head from one of those irresponsibly-conceived toys.

Winter brought the thrills of tobogganing down the hilly road outside the farmyard or on the slopes in the field past the mill. Philip and I would pant eagerly back up the hill for a fresh start, to be made either singly or riding in tandem. Later I experienced the pride of possessing my very own toboggan, of pine-fresh wood and fitted with gleaming runners made by the local blacksmith. Those were days of downward rushes through the freezing clean air, with the sun striking ice-blue diamonds of light from the crisp, virgin snow.

I never managed to attend the famous Nottingham Goose Fair until after we left Newbound Mill Farm, but there was another annual amusement fair only three miles down the road at Hardwick. Here could be found assembled such standard equipment for excitement, spending-spree jollity and mouth-gaping curiosity as probably owed more to Coney Island than Merry England. Garish peacocks, bounding horses and outmoded limousines circled round blaring, automated organs; male and female daredevils hurtled on mats down the giddy, spiral tower of the helter-skelter; beefy, stetsoned cowgirls in short skirts postured invitingly by the box-office of the Wild West show; the weight guesser ran lecherous hands over scandalised or willing ladies; and dull thuds or ringing clangs signalled hits or misses at the coconut shies. There was little need to ask the way to that raucous, mushroom town of caravans, tents and sweaty press of humanity – simply follow the noise by day or glare by night for a rollicking good time!

Those fairground organs were second cousins to the barrel organs trundled around towns and villages to earn their seedy looking owners a copper or two by short, hand-cranked recitals of such current favourites as *Peggy O'Neil* or *Bye Bye Blackbird*. Sometimes there would be a pathetic looking little monkey dressed in a short jacket, always seeming to be scanning the onlookers for someone he never found.

Piano playing was a family accomplishment, Mother, Hilda and Philip each having learned to play, whilst I foolishly resisted several attempts to persuade me into taking lessons myself. It was only a few years before I began bitterly to regret this for the rest of my life, but although I am still deeply fond of music I never quite made the break to learn a particular instrument. I have in truth often fantasised over being a violin virtuoso, humbly acknowledging a standing applause as I incline my immaculately clad figure to an enraptured audience following an inspired rendering of some dream-like concerto. As it was, I got no further than watching Philip practice *The Bluebells of Scotland* at the piano, to the steady tick-tock of a metronome.

In addition to music and lots of reading, we absorbed other quotas of culture by attending evening lectures at Pleasley. These edifying sessions were on a variety of subjects, though travel was the top favourite. For us, even a dry-sounding affair like 'Exploring the Lower Reaches of the Limpopo' could prove to be absorbing when supported by magic-lantern slides. As often as not the talk would be delivered by some sobersides missionary, his assistant generally managing to get at least one slide upside down; on one unforgettable occasion a picture of a scantily-clad young lady managed to get mixed up with the more serious subject matter, raising subdued titters from the audience and embarrassed coughs from the lecturer as matters were hurried by put right. Heaven knows what guilty secret lay behind that little contretemps!

Mother was a staunch supporter of the local Band of Hope, a teetotal organisation dedicated to persuading young and old against the evils of accepting even one glass of beer or tot of gin. Those crafty zealots promoted their cause deviously, starting each evening with a talk on some subject far removed from their real objective, the latter being broached when everyone had been further softened up by

tea and sticky buns. Frank and I were virtually detailed by Mother to attend, and we would trudge to Pleasley on winter nights carrying a hurricane lamp and chewing creamy toffees. One evening I was invited onto the platform by the lecturer to help him uncoil and exhibit a vivid-patterned snake skin – a proud and brave moment for me. I have to state that this early indoctrination failed to make any lasting impression on me, for I still enjoy froth-topped pints which refresh those parts no lecturer could hope to reach!

In those pioneering days of wireless, the romance of the Morse Code gripped me at one time, forming the basis for a game which I devised for my friend Leonard and I to play. We sited ourselves at opposite ends of a field, each equipped with an empty sheep-dip drum and engine-oil can which gave high and low-pitched notes when struck with a stick. With our codes pasted-up on cardboard for reference, we passed laconic messages such as "Icebergs ahead!", answered by "Will make full speed astern", or simply "Going home for dinner".

When searching around for some new diversion, my imagination was sometimes fuelled by adverts in boys' magazines, generally on the lines of "Amaze your chums. Send only is 6d." I acquired one booklet entitled *Hypnotism Simplified,* but no amount of trance-inducing pendulums or intonations of "You are feeling drowsy now – *sleep. . . sleep. . . sleep*" had the slightest effect on Hilda or Philip, and the cat was probably tired before I tried it on her anyway!

My attempts at ventriloquism were slightly more encouraging, though no matter how I tried to vary the voices produced by the device I had purchased (a small disc held against the tongue), the results all had a constipated Donald Duck sound about them.

I suppose that conjuring was the best of my novelty turns, for I decided that rather than rely on sleight of hand I would let chemicals work for me. As a result, I could with the greatest of ease and without fail turn water into wine, change white roses to pink and make written names reappear phoenix-like from their ashes rubbed onto my bare arm.

Amongst those tricks and novelties I must not forget to mention the magic beans (Mexican, I believe) bought for a penny or two at joke shops. These intriguing seeds would respond to slight warming by repeatedly jumping a good inch or so off the palm of the hand. I learned later on that these caperings are due to no magical powers on the part of the beans, as they are caused by the bad-tempered somersaults of a resident bug, showing his disapproval at having his sleep disturbed.

16

MISCHIEF AFOOT

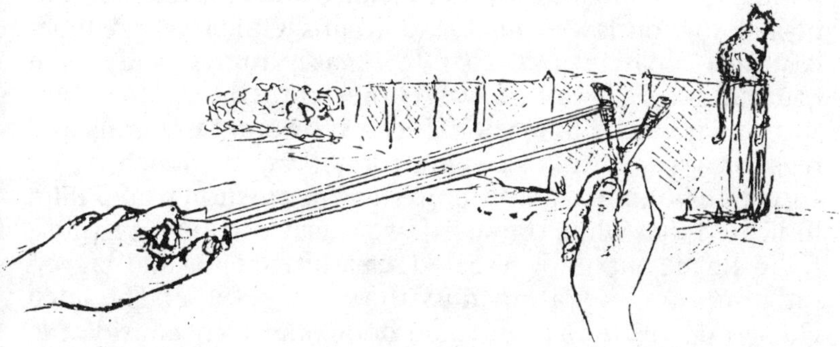

Naughty boys (and girls!) must be very trying to parents who have more serious worries to contend with than wondering what the next puerile prank will be. No wonder patience gives out at times and Mum or Dad lets fly at the somewhat less than angelic offspring who only a decade ago lay gurgling in his cot, or sucking his thumb like the sweet little cherub he was. ("Isn't he a little darling! Whoever could dream of hurting such poor little mites?"). And so it was with us, even to the point where at times Philip was deemed to have been as equally involved as myself in some escapade or other. The classic situation would be where Mother had informed Father who had promised to do something about it, and now he stood on the far side of the living room table, slowly unbuckling his belt and eyeing us fixedly as he asked "Now then, which of you wants it first?" – a rhetorical question if ever there was! There would be a slow, ritual circling of the table then a sudden dash by one of we culprits, with Mother blocking the boltholes. Pure farce!

To be walloped for clearly doing wrong is one thing, but physical punishment on top of severe pain resulting from boyish fun is simply not playing the game. It happened like this. Philip and I had been playing at Wild West goodies and baddies, he being the good-guy sheriff whilst I was that son-of-a-skunk outlaw from Dead Man's Gulch (good type-casting!). After a desperate chase round the town (outbuildings), finally I was cornered in the saloon (bin-room) where the able sheriff securely bound my arms and legs with rope, till I resembled nothing so much as an Egyptian mummy. A muttered stage instruction from Philip indicated that while the sheriff was away organising a posse to hustle me out of town seated rearwards-facing and gagged on a mustang, it was my duty to try and escape. The latch clicked down on the bin-room door, and I lay considering the details of my escape; soon I had somehow regained my feet, still with arms and legs tightly bound. Inch by inch I shuffled to the door, lifted the latch with my nose and after more tactical manoeuvrings stood poised at the threshold, overlooking the yard. There was a low step down to the cobbled path which proved to be my undoing, for after a brief off-balance tottering I toppled forward and took those cobbles right on the chin, sustaining a painful gash, two teeth rattled clean out of their sockets and an Old Glory display of stars and stripes. My screams brought Father running up, but after releasing me the expected sympathy turned out to be a thrashing with the rope's end. The sheriff? – nowhere to be found!

The apparent injustice of the foregoing episode is more than offset by my deep guilt in respect of the egg throwing experiments; but I talk in riddles, so here is the full story. In one of those boys' magazines which seem to keep cropping up in my stories, I had read of the remarkable strength of an egg when subjected to lengthwise pressure. Now without going into the boring details of my immature, country bumpkin reasoning. I decided to carry out my own laboratory investigations of this phenomenon. They could more accurately be described as field tests, for I would climb onto a haystack and hurl a succession of eggs end-over-end into the field, watching intently to decide which of them struck the ground at the required angle and then hurrying down to see whether or not they remained intact. The innocent hens probably got the blame for what must have appeared to be a sudden decline in their egg yield. In the light of all this and in respect of injustice, I should ask myself "Who will cast the first stone?"

I will rub my own nose a little further into the dirt by recalling another irresponsible practice of mine when called on from time to time to give my baby sister Gladys an airing in her pram. I discovered that the faster I walked with her the more she seemed to like it, so I progressed first to gentle trotting and then to running, often propelling her several yards ahead with a good shove and then running to take hold of the pram again. She would chuckle and kick her tiny feet excitedly at the fun of it all, so one evening I went a step further. It was on the way back from Teversal village to where I had wheeled Gladys to show her off to my headmistress, Miss Clarke. There was a steep hill which started by the school and ran down towards a little bridge, so I let the pram run on a few yards then waved as usual and ran to catch up with it – or so I had intended, for that innocuous-looking, gravity-powered vehicle soon proved that it could gather speed faster than I could! Baby Gladys apparently thought this just another game, laughing away as though it were the best thing after syrup on her dummy. With me running pell-mell in worried pursuit, the pram ricocheted off the bridge then soft-landed in a hedgerow, Gladys still chuckling fit to burst, unaware of the fact that only divine intervention had saved her from a nasty accident.

My cousin Frank's inexpert fooling around with a sheep-dunking pole once landed him, his elder brother Tom, Philip and myself all in trouble with both sets of parents. While the adults were gossiping and tea drinking in the house one Sunday afternoon on a pleasant but cool spring day, we boys amused ourselves with games which centred around the mill-pond. Two long T-poles were always stored nearby, ready for when the sheep were pushed repeatedly under the water during their annual wash in the pond prior to shearing. Philip and I were used to playing with those unwieldy devices, and presently Frank fell to copying us in pole-vault-like feints at the pond, but then he was an inexperienced townie. With rising confidence he made one over-ambitious run and leap with the pole, taking him soaring up over the point of no return and into the pond! Frank surfaced and waded to the side with arms held aloft and covered in pondweed, like Neptune looking for a wash and brush-up. We dredged out his spectacles and stripped him off, telling him to run around the field to get dry and keep warm. Meanwhile we laundered his suit in the by now muddied water, with forlorn hopes that the stains might not show when it was dried. As Frank jogged around in the cool air like a sprinter warming-up at a nudist athletics meeting, we suddenly heard our respective mothers approaching round the outbuildings to see how their lads were getting on (gathering cowslips for Mother?). Quick as lightning we pushed Frank into the old mill, snatched his drying clothing off the wall and threw it out of sight near the bank, then mooched around sheepishly, pretending to admire a waterhen's nest. Now mums are not easily fooled under such circumstances, and on receiving evasive replies as to Frank's whereabouts they looked around and spotted his clothing on the bank – the lad had done away with himself, worried by his exam results! The game was up, and a shivering Frank emerged from the mill with his hands cupped in the regulation fig-leaf position. A good time was not had by all!

Although in those days we did not seem to have quite the same problems associated with growing up as we do today, possibly this was partly due to the word 'teenager' not yet having been coined. But then the natural instincts were so repressed by Victorian prudery (cold showers for youths and buckets of water for dogs) that who could say what lay beneath the mill-pond calm of human deep waters? I am thinking in particular of sister Hilda, contrasting her utter respectability in later life with her transgressions around the age of sixteen – she was a brown-paper smoker! Not content with her own depravity, she dragged her two young brothers into her shameful little ring of vice, luring us to the shrubbery for furtive puffs and coughs as reprehensible as those other goings-on behind school bicycle sheds. Our early sessions left us rather surprised that our elders found such pleasure in the habit, so we experimented with brands other than the original coarse wrapping-paper variety, working our way through blue sugar-bags to the Turkish flavour of corrugated cardboard. I believe the dried raspberry leaves clinched matters for Hilda, as she never smoked again.

That boyhood attraction for playing with fire taught me a useful lesson early on in life, for I nearly burned down the blacksmith's shop. The blacksmith was a kindly man and would raise no objection to children peeping in to watch him produce pyrotechnic displays from the coke fire by fierce puffs from the wheezing bellows, or fashion horseshoes as his anvil rang out across the village. One day there was a small pool of petrol lying amongst the cobbles by the open doorway of the smithy, spilled by some careless motorist when filling up from a can. Behind the blacksmith's back an older, knowing lad dipped a long stick in the petrol and lit it at the fire, then ran outside with this plaything. I followed suit, and for a minute or so enjoyed running around the yard like an Olympic torch bearer. As the flame started to die down, what more sensible thing to do than replenish it from the pool – Whoomphhh! I ran around terrified with my eyelashes singed and my hair on fire, though quickly rescued by the blacksmith.

Father had a double-barrelled shotgun which I longed to use, though that was of course strictly forbidden to me. One day when I was eleven years old and everyone else was away, an opportunity for using the gun presented itself which I believed warranted my breaking the rules, for several times I saw a large rat in and out of the bin-room. Should I or should I not – yes! I loaded the gun and crept to a corner overlooking that verminous activity and crouched down in readiness for the next sighting. When it came, I pulled the trigger and straightway found myself flat on my back with a badly bruised jaw and shoulder, coupled with a gash near my thumb where the hammer had dug in with the recoil. However, all this was as nothing when I saw the dead body of the thief lying by the bin-room door, which had itself been peppered with shot. I could not resist telling Father when he returned, and strangely enough I was not punished, and indeed was from then on allowed to use the gun occasionally by being sent to shoot a rabbit for dinner.

On the subject of shooting let me tell you a story of which I should not be over-proud, but then it begs to be told and after all I was only ten at the time. I had been lent an air rifle by a neighbouring farmer who, I may say with hindsight, ought to have known better. Having run out of lead pellets I first experimented with grains of wheat and then selected a live target – the bull. Secure behind a five-barred gate, I took aim and fired at what proved to be his Achilles heel, with dramatic results. There was a quick shudder and arching of the back, a pause, then a powerful exhalation of breath like the first move of a steam train leaving a platform. A slight inclination of the head and rolling of the eyes led me to

suspect that the outraged animal was about to charge the perpetrator of this affront to his masculinity, but to my surprise and relief the only further outcome was a short trickle of tears down his noble cheeks. He had taken his punishment like a man! You could reflect on whether his story might have been passed down through generations of other young bulls, but the anatomical implications of the affair raise doubts as to whether such progeny every existed. You might also ask whether or not this story is just a load of – well, shall we say nonsense. My answer is that I did indeed fire that shot at the bull, and though the ballistic qualities of a grain of wheat are in doubt, nevertheless I am, and have always been an excellent marksman.

Our persian cat Fluff must have thought it a very strange household at times, for in addition to the near-roasting she had received in the oven, she was involved in another highly unfortunate affair. She was snoozing by the fireside one peaceful afternoon when she and I were in the house alone, my way of passing the time being to play with my clockwork railway engine. Tiring of runing the engine round and round the same boring little circle of track, I wound it fully and sent it across the floor on course for Fluff as she dreamed of fat mice, handsome toms or whatever pussycats do daydream about. As the engine touched her there was a split-second reaction, for the cat flew off the hearth and screamed around the room as though demented – running up one long curtain then leaping across to the other like a flying fox – her cavortings being so rapid and erratic that I could not assess what her problem was. With one last screech she shot into the kitchen accompanied by a strange clanging noise – the hapless animal had been trying to shake off the toy engine as its cogwheel bit into her tail like a ferret hanging on to its prey. No blandishments of cream or jellied rabbit's legs could ever fully restore that disillusioned creature's faith in her sadistic owners.

17

LOVE'S SPRINGTIME

As I draft this chapter, smug satisfaction laps over me on re-reading the heading. What I shrewd fellow I was to distill that sweet feeling into two words! The Bard himself could scarcely have beaten that – well in English anyway. But wait – it may evoke the feeling, but what about the detail? That heading refuses to go away, so I must make the best of my sparse material, after all, there is unlikely to be much earth-moving between the ages of seven plus and eleven plus.

Childhood loves are not like the later variety. Cupid inflicts only flesh wounds on us, painful for a short time, but healing quickly without the sensitive scars left by encounters as we get older. Only pleasant though blurred-edge memories remain, unspoilt by the enlightenments that follow deeper strolls into the Garden of Eden.

My first recollection of young, loving feelings concerns Jean and I admiring the brilliance of morning stars one frosty dawn; but here I cheat a little as I was only two at the time and she was fifteen, being our maid in better-off days before my present stories. However, equally romantic was my first crush at Teversal school, for the object of my affections was a charcoal-burner's daughter! Fittingly, I was a woodcutter, and with my arm around her waist our love blossomed as I sang "I know a bank whereon the wild thyme blows." She could have replied "Yes, but Mum's warned me about boys like you!", but then this was a family show, being the school play at Christmas. Dorothy was a colliery engineer's daughter, darkly Cleopatra-like and dressed in deep-red velvet – rich ingredients for stirring the passions of a seven-year-old.

Red velvet seemed to attract me, as at least two other early loves wore that material. One was Betty, who I saw only two or three times when her family visited us from a farm some distance away. The time I remember best was another Christmas, when Mother lit a fire in the 'spare room' downstairs, and we both played happily together there for a couple of hours. Funnily enough, Betty also was dark, and had the looks of a young 'serpent of Old Nile'. Cleopatra, red velvet, Christmas - was there some Freudian connection?

An incident during a visit to friends at yet another farm should have served as an early warning on the temptations of the flesh: it proved far too pleasurable for that. With parents busy gossiping in the house, daughter Molly fetched me out to the paddock where she and her girl-friend had made a secret hide-out in the recess of a haystack. There was instant rapport between the friend and myself, and when Molly left us for whatever reason, we fell into rough-and-tumble games which brought us into fleeting but delicious contacts of hands, bare arms and legs. This was heaven, and taking boldness as my guide I planned to try a kiss. Suddenly she was gone – leaving a void of disappointment which (not withstanding my earlier dissertation) still hurts whenever I recall that brief encounter. Sadly, I never even learned her name.

Another charming temptress was my water-nymph Olive. Here our relationship was more of the Pyramus and Thisby type, as we were separated by a thick stone wall. She was slightly older than me, around thirteen, and on weekend summer afternoons would come from Pleasley with a coterie of male admirers, to paddle in the stream by the old bridge below the farm. I would lean over the bridge wall, looking down at her as barefooted and with frock tucked in knickers she picked her way daintily across the ford. She knew she was being watched both from below and above, and made the most of her stage appearances, archly darting quick glances up at me. She broke my Freudian rule, as she was fair, with a swathe of hair held becomingly off the winsome face by a tortoiseshell slide. If only that tiresome bodyguard had not been with her, Olive and I might have become better acquainted. In the event, our family moved from Newbound Mill the following spring, so bang went another budding romance!

From as early as we could repeat nursery rhymes, we boys were told how different we were from little girls. The definitive jingle went: "What are little girls made of? Sugar and spice, and all that's nice; that's what little girls are made of", whereas our basic materials were said to be "frogs, snails and puppy-dogs' tails". That sounded straightforward enough, but did not appear to be borne out by the facts. Most of us could not deny being 'dirty little boys', but on the other hand we did not find all little girls 'sweet'. There

were also unexplained differences apart from outward appearances. For example, why was it far pleasanter to touch or hold hands with Jill or Mary than with Tom, Dick or Harry? And why were boys' frocks changed in favour of trousers from about the age of three onwards?

Rumours regarding those matters abounded and sometimes conflicted, though it seemed that the older children often knew more than they were prepared to divulge. Ah well, it could not be that important, and in any case there were still birds' nests to be found and coloured marbles to swap. But the curiosity remained, and would be re-fired from time to time by tell-tale girls of our age leaking information received from elder sisters.

There were rumours that the older girls were willing to give biology lessons to we younger boys, using female infant tots press-ganged into acting as live models by temporarily divesting them of their modesty. However, my real introduction to this subject had to await my undergrad days in the University of Life.

Boy-girl liasons of all age-groups were being formed and broken all the time, seeming to get more intense and interesting the older one became. These attachments were widely advertised by chalkings, scratchings or carvings on desks, walls, school paths or trees. The announcements usually took the form of initialled hearts pierced by Cupid's arrow, the statement "A.B. goes with C.D.," or a simple "EF=GH", as though the affair could be reduced to an algebraic formula. Changes of heart meant scribbled erasions, though hearts on oak-trees were not so easily amended. Some years ago, on re-visiting Teversal I was touched to discover one or two of these records of young love dated around a century ago, still etched on a bridge over the stream there.

One day I was puzzled when someone pointed out my initials linked with those of a slightly older girl, chalked on the school wall near the entrance porch. I had not long to wait for further developments, as within minutes the girl in question passed by with her friend and slipped a note into my hand. It read "Will you go with me? D." I was honoured, and accepted the invitation, though apprehensive as to whether or not a younger lad like me could match her expectations. The note was treasured and secreted inside my hollow pot bulldog – the guardian of other secrets too. Some years later and after we had both left the area, the sad news reached me across the country that she had been killed in a riding accident.

It was sad that at Teversal School there were so many young girls whose attractiveness was masked by the results of poverty and sometimes obvious neglect. They were thin, ill-dressed, grimy, with unstyled and unkempt hair, yet sometimes their natural attributes shone through and at least partly overcame those handicaps. The youngest ones may not have felt the situation quite so much, but as they grew older it must have hurt to realise they were so disadvantaged. Some of them looked quite sad, in fact on looking back I could say that dejection was the keyword to describe their expression. One girl in particular who I clearly remember wore the plainest of black, sleeveless dresses, shapeless, absolutely threadbare, and unrelieved by any sort of pleating or other enhancements whatsoever. It was obvious that she wore nothing underneath, nor did she have stockings or socks, and for footwear she wore plimsolls almost in shreds. Yet in spite of these humiliations she remained pleasant though downcast.

Another girl I remember was disadvantaged in rather a different way, though it was still concerned with general turnout. (As a male chauvinist, I might call it general presentation and wrapping of the goods!). Her mother must have been living in the past, for she sent young Anonymous to school dressed as though for the role of Alice in Wonderland, even down to those juvenile unmentionables with gathered-in frills peeping from below the hemline of her dress. Perhaps mum was a misogamist, determined that her daughter should remain firmly on the shelf right from the start.

At the other end of the scale, there were a few girls who never failed to delight we young romeos with their looks, dress, cleanliness, personality and general allure. But we males never learn, for I remember fighting a bloody-nosed battle with one of my best friends over just such a budding sorceress; I emerged the victor, only to have the object of my affections opt for the vanquished after all. It has been said that none but the brave deserve the fair, though it would appear that to deserve is one thing, but to actually carry off the prize can be a different matter entirely.

In the light of that last anecdote, perhaps it is the sour-grapes of jealousy that prompts me to recall that, after all, it may be better to travel than to arrive. Certainly some of the little romantic journies were pleasant enough, like passing coded notes to the loved one via a relay of hands under the cover of desk-tops, pockets and dresses, eagerly awaiting a reply by the same route and hopefully by return of post. Would she or wouldn't she? These messages always risked interception by the headmistress, Miss Clarke, success resulting in her reading them and reprimanding the culprit. Perhaps she had her own youthful memories capable of being stirred by those notes, as during singing lessons she always joined in the romantic songs with a great deal of feeling.

That secret note-passing partly made up for a rule that there should be no fraternization with the other sex at playtime, and so the girls' playground was strictly out-of-bounds to us. I will not pretend that these regulations were observed anything like fully, as there was a loophole difficult to seal, for we could communicate via the back-to-back boys' and girls' lavatories. However, this was not an ideal trysting place, speech being distorted through the wall and the general atmosphere being somewhat less than conducive to romance.

In that matter of lovenotes, one sophistication was the writing of cryptic letters across the sealed flap, such as S.W.A.L.K. (Sealed with a loving kiss) or I.L.Y.O. (I love you only). Should you receive one of these which you could not understand, then the wisdom of some fourteen-year-old sibyl had to be tapped for an interpretation.

A far more appropriate setting for country lads and lasses get-togethers was of course the countryside itself, and one of my pleasantest memories concerns just that. One summer afternoon when we came out of Sunday school, several of us paired off for a walk along a footpath through the fields. The idea was that we should receive instruction from Sylvia, she being one of the oldest, on the general behaviours and deportment expected of courting couples. This short course started with kissing lessons behind a large bush, we being called there one at a time as though it was a game of postman's knock. That proved to be an agreeable enough start, and was followed by being shown how to walk with arms around waists while keeping in step, so as to be in unison from an ambulatory as well as an amatory point of view. The sun shone, the hedgerows bloomed and the birds chirruped their roundelays. What more fitting way could there be to walk into the sunset of these rhapsodical recollections?

18

EVENING REFLECTIONS

My old headmistress taught me that every 'composition' should have a beginning, the meaty part and an end, so I will finish by running an eye over my chapter headings and expressing a few views on how I see things as having changed since I was a boy.

The general scene of those boyhood times remains almost untouched by the years, for after an uninspiring run-in from the motorway this spring, suddenly I felt like that hose-and-doublet clad prince who broke through a thicket to discover an enchanted castle, arrested in time. The sleepy village is just as before, and the farmstead as approached from

Teversal looks as it did each afternoon when I returned from school.

As to the *dramatis personae* of the scenes played there so long ago, Father and Mother both left the stage at a fairly ripe old age, having lived life to the full but without material benefits commensurate with their efforts. My brother Philip died relatively young, after a career in the Royal Navy which latterly included a spell on Lord Louis Mountbatten's personal staff and other name-dropping experiences such as lunch with Marshal Tito. Sisters Hilda and Gladys live on with their own memories, but our cheerful helper Frank ploughed his last furrow many years ago. Apart from the pets and livestock (God bless them), that just leaves myself. Much of my life was spent in the Royal Air Force, but that is another story I hope to tell elsewhere.

For we who remain, our daily routines are so smoothed at every turn by labour-saving devices, gadgetry and materials that it is difficult to imagine how our parents managed to do anything more than simply keep the household running. From our awakening by an electronic bleep, through a centrally-heated day of vacuum-cleaned housework, microwave-cooked convenience foods, automatically-washed clothing, telephone calls and car trips, until finally the light spot shrinks and dies on the TV screen at bedtime, we are cosseted beyond the comprehension of any time traveller who should drop in from the 1920s.

Water pumps are now isolated-cottage oddities, constant hot water has rendered the term bathnight obsolete, and WCs really are water closets. Illness no longer holds so many uncertainties nor the worries of paying doctors' bills, and we are treated with complex drugs in place of country simples.

Most of our cherished props of everyday life have gone – the furniture, hardware and ornaments – though our tendency is to replace them with similar items, often as reminders rather than for actual use; indeed the public in general cannot find enough old houses or antiques to satisfy the craving for such things, so they watch, listen and read about it all.

Modern clothing reflects several trends which would have seemed strange at Newbound Mill Farm: we wear very few hand-me-downs and clothes are mostly of synthetic materials, lightweight, easily cleaned and so durable that we get fed up with wearing a particular item. Here the rag trade steps in to mop up the surplus cash which so many of us have, but few will admit, after meeting our essential needs, (This generation does not have to spend hours making rugs from worn-out clothing.)

The question of today's relative affluence leads me to reflect on how hard we children had to work for our weekly few pence, whereas now parents seem happy to part with £2 or more so that a bored child can loll around watching some moronic video. I can only say that I would back our form of upbringing against theirs.

The recent new owners of our farm, Mr and Mrs Lepley, kindly showed my wife and I around since I drafted this book, and I was delighted to find that in spite of many alterations to the house my bedroom remains virtually unaltered since I used my braces as a catapult. Most of the farm buildings stand unchanged except for one or two demolitions, which sadly include the old water-mill. However, I have no doubt that descendants of the sparrows, mice and spiders of my boyhood years live on in what remains. The fruit trees have all gone, taking with them those lazy hours in hammocks and the perils of cherry stealing.

After that nose-around of the farmstead I strolled to the bridge and looked to see if my initials still showed amongst the hundreds carved there, wondering also what happened to my water-nymph Olive, then it was on to lunch with other old friends at Teversal village – sisters Margaret and René together with their cousins Jessie and Dorothy. We swapped old memories and more recent tales of how all that young human material had developed in later life – n'er-do-wells, successes, rogues, saints and sinners. Following a look at the old school (now converted into a pair of houses) and standing for a peaceful minute or two in the churchyard by the grave of my old headmistress, Miss Clarke (1870-1955), it was time to go.

Prior to that meet-up I had already tracked down two other friends from those years – sisters Sylvia and Pat – and viewed things through the rose-tinted spectacles which Time so kindly provides us with.

How easy it was to make those car journies to see old friends and places, though for sheer pleasure in the act of travelling give me a leisurely horse and trap ride along a country road in preference to a tensed-up rat race up the M1 or around the M25; even the smoke, steam and cinders in the eye of an old-fashioned railway journey would be better than that.

I notice that somehow I have skipped the heading relating to food. Sadly, probably many of those who stand at pub bars pontificating on this snob-value subject have never experienced the satisfaction of growing, picking and cooking their own food, nor the pleasures of anticipating each variety in its season. For them, the deep-freeze, tin and packet have replaced the kitchen garden and orchard, and why bother with Mrs Beeton when there is cook-in-a-bag or a quick trip to the Chinese takeaway.

Fortunately there is still the countryside to be enjoyed, though it shrinks a little each year and is constantly threatened by various poisons and other abuses. One difference from my childhood days is the number of old footpaths that have been closed by falling into disuse and being misappropriated by some of the farmers. But then who troubles to walk across the fields when there is a car outside the door.

Present-day pleasures are almost as artificial and pre-packed as the food, with very little home-grown stuff either; they seem to come in three basic flavours – sex, sport and violence, each laced with alcohol. We do not take our music sheets to parties any more for there is unlikely to be a piano there, and in any case it is far easier to obtain instant culture by slipping a casette into the music-centre.

There is plenty of opportunity for mischief – telephone kiosks to be vandalised, old ladies to be mugged or rival spectators to be kicked in the head at soccer matches. When you tire of messing on your own doorstep, a day trip across the Channel will enable you to show the flag abroad by smashing up some French or Belgian waterfront bar.

Finally there is love, where once again everything is made easy, with abortion and divorce on tap if anything goes wrong. Postman's Knock has given way to borrowing Dad's car for petting in a layby, and furtive telephone calls at his expense are more convenient (though less romantic) than secret love-letters on perfumed note paper.

What does it all add up to? To condense my view into a few words, I believe that in my lifetime we have made technological and material advances far beyond the understanding of the average citizen, yet we are no further forward either in the pursuit of happiness or in getting along with our fellow human beings and other creatures – in fact we have slipped back.

I would like to end these recollections by quoting a few words from one of our favourite songs which rang out at Teversal school from time to time:

The cuckoo is a pretty bird,
She singeth as she flies.

Like the cuckoo, we are birds of passage in Time, enjoying ourselves at the expense of others.

* * *